As Luck Would Have It
My Exile in France and Mexico
Recollections and Stories

Studies in Austrian Literature, Culture and Thought

Biography, Autobiography, Memoirs Series

General Editors:

Jorun B. Johns
Richard H. Lawson

BRUNO SCHWEBEL

AS LUCK WOULD HAVE IT

MY EXILE IN FRANCE AND MEXICO

Recollections and Stories

Translated and with an Afterword by

Michael Winkler

Ariadne Press
Riverside, California

Ariadne Press would like to express its appreciation to the Bundesministerium für Unterricht, Kunst und Kultur for assistance in publishing this book.

.KUNST

Translated from the German *Das andere Glück.*
Erinnerungen und Erzählungen
© 2004 Theodor Kramer Gesellschaft, Wien

Library of Congress Cataloging-in-Publication Data

Schwebel, Bruno.
 [Andere Glück. English]
 As luck would have it : my exile in France and Mexico, recollections and stories / Bruno Schwebel ; translated and with an afterword by Michael Winkler.
   p. cm. -- (Studies in Austrian literature, culture, and thought. Biography, autobiography, memoirs series)
 Includes bibliographical references.
 ISBN 1-57241-157-0 (978-1-57241-157-9 : alk. paper)
 1. Schwebel, Bruno. 2. World War, 1939-1945—Refugees—Mexico—Biography. I. Winkler, Michael, 1937- II. Title

PQ7298.29.C54Z46 2008
863'.64--dc22

2008004479

Cover Design
Art Director: George McGinnis
Designer: Beth A. Steffel

Copyright 2008
by Ariadne Press
270 Goins Court
Riverside, CA 92507

All rights reserved.
No part of this publication may be reproduced or transmitted
in any form or by any means without formal permission.
Printed in the United States of America.
ISBN 1-57241-157-0; 978-1-57241-157-9

Table of Contents

Preface 1

Chapter 1:   Vienna 5
Chapter 2:   Neulengbach 17
Chapter 3:   Neulengbach in the 1920s 26
Chapter 4:   The Hössingers 33
Chapter 5:   Purkersdorf 39
Chapter 6:   The Escape to France 48
Chapter 7:   Paris 53
Chapter 8:   Montmorency 60
Chapter 9:   Flight from Paris 68
Chapter 10: Montauban, the Beginning 73
Chapter 11: Preparations in Montauban 80
Chapter 12: Mademoiselle de Fauche — *Story* 87
Chapter 13: Fleeing to Lisbon 93
Chapter 14: The Crossing 99
Chapter 15: Mexico, the First Weeks 105
Chapter 16: The First Years in Mexico 115
Chapter 17: "Yonkes" and Other Ruins — *Story* 123
Chapter 18: The Guarura — *Story* 128
Chapter 19: Acclimating to Mexico 133
Chapter 20: The Evolution of La Cangreja — *Story* 141
Chapter 21: Student Years 144
Chapter 22: Polish Opening — *Story* 157
Chapter 23: The Other Michaela — *Story* 160
Chapter 24: The Old Woman — *Story* 165
Chapter 25: Putting Down Roots in Mexico 170

Chapter 26: El Señor Lector – *Story* 175
Chapter 27: Anne Belle and the Birds – *Story* 179
Chapter 28: The Doctor – *Story* 183
Chapter 29: The Decision 188
Chapter 30: Returning 194

Notes 201

Afterword by Michael Winkler 220

Preface

Over the last few years, I've been engaging my memory and my computer – sole witnesses of my emotions – with the life I have lived, first in Spanish and, with much help, during the translation of these memoirs into German.

With tears in my eyes, I go to see the places of my childhood in order to unravel the tangle of my recollections. It is a peculiar and surprising experience to realize how suppressed emotions, even after so many years, come back to life. With a heavy heart, I thought of the times spent at the Haaghof in Neulengbach with my grandfather and with my Jewish family, remembering their fate. Writing made me live through the years in France again and again, with the unforgettable Red Falcons and the other children at the home in Montmorency, the flight from Paris ahead of the German army, the uncertainty of being separated from my mother and my father. I gave my pent-up emotions free rein, their weight apparently unwilling to search for relief.

Next came the hours when I was occupied with my Mexican life. Nostalgia let me bring back the experiences of sixty-two years. The reality of Mexico was, is, and remains overwhelming – my relationship with my immediate and my extended family, with my schoolmates and other friends, my close ties to this country that offered me a refuge, a new home, security, and a very promising future.

On every return to Austria I see prosperity and contentedness, and I admire the social safety net people have built for themselves. I am proud that my father's and my uncle's socialist commitment has contributed to this success in some small measure. My suspicion toward my Austrian compatriots continues to diminish, even though an urgent need to pelt the slap-in-the-face man in the Prater to my heart's desire is impossible to bring under control. Little by little, I learn how to differentiate. I find new friends, devour desserts, and walk through my old home country with open eyes. But the nostalgic pleasure of biting into a pickle on the Danube meadows, of listening to the sizzle of a bottle of soda pop during a Sunday excursion up the Kahlenberg, or of discovering a large parasol mushroom among the leafage of the Vienna Woods is something no longer granted me.

DEDICATION IN MEMORIAM

My parents
My brother
My murdered Jewish family
Don Gilberto Bosques, Mexican Consul General in Marseille during the times of war

Thank you, Christian Kloyber, for your commitment and friendship

Bruno Schwebel (2004)

4

Chapter 1

VIENNA

At the very same moment that President Portes Gil shouted "Viva México!" three times and a huge crowd celebrating the national holiday on the Zócalo added its "and to hell with the *gachupines*" and all the bells were tolling, my mother was crossing Allerheiligenplatz in Vienna on her way to the hospital. Her labor had started. It was a Sunday – September 16, 1928 – rather early in the morning, and she was in a hurry. Her water broke in the park. When she arrived at the clinic – today it's the Lorenz Böhler Emergency Hospital – I was just about to see the light of day. Yes, even then I made a dry impression. Sometimes I imagine that some of my chromosomes were left behind when she spilled her water in that park. And who knows what has become of them after seventy-five years.

We lived in public housing, in a place known as Janecek-Hof, built in the mid-twenties for government employees. It stands at 30 Donaueschingen-Straße in Brigittenau, Vienna's 20th district. Many of these buildings, named in those years mostly after left-leaning European leaders (Karl Marx, Friedrich Engels, Otto Bauer, Viktor Adler, and others), were constructed during three generations of socialist city government. They provided a home for some sixty-five thousand families. After I had to leave Austria in 1938, I have returned to Janecek-Hof on three occasions and every time found it clean and in good repair, quite in contrast to public housing in Mexico. From our apartment on the third floor, we could look into one of the inner courtyards with its patch of lawn, swing, and sand box for the children. Nowadays these buildings have an elevator. On every return visit to my childhood, I see myself trying to cover three steps in one leap or sliding down the banisters. (It was only years later – in my nightmares about being chased by brownshirts with swastikas – that I managed to jump from one floor to the next in a single bound.) On the other side of the street was the laundry house for the women of our neighborhood. This is where my mother too, shrouded in clouds of hot steam, washed diapers and garnered – I am very sure of that – a good deal of praise for her two cute little boys: Helmut, two years old, and myself. And I recall a tongue twister I memorized as a child: "Wir Wiener Wäscheweiber wollen weiße Wäsche waschen, wenn wir wüßten, wo warmes, weiches Wasser wär." (We Viennese washerwomen wash white woolies while we wonder why warm wellwater waves whirl wildly.)

Brigittenau was and continues to be a district with a largely working-class population, the so-called proletariat, a term barely remembered these days. Many guest workers live there now, most of them Turks. On my last visit, as I was ambling across Allerheiligenplatz, which is only two blocks away from Janecek-Hof, women in Islamic robes looked me over with indifferent, though not unfriendly glances, seeing that I was a stranger in their world. Men in dark outfits had gathered in small groups, smoking and chatting. I saw no joy in their faces, a few children excepted.

My mother, Therese Hössinger, called Resi by all who knew her, hailed from the village of Tausendblum near Neulengbach, some forty minutes by train from Vienna's Westbahnhof. Many of her relatives worked for the Railroad in jobs like conductor, ticket agent, and inspector. My Catholic mother met my Jewish father during his political and cultural activities in this region. She converted to the Mosaic faith in February 1924, assuming the new name of Ruth, and they were married on May 2 of that same year.

The super at Janecek-Hof, a man named Leitner, had a daughter, Anna, who was a little younger than my mother. She was a dancer and without doubt my first great love. This may sound exaggerated but passion took hold of me when I was not more than three years old. When we had to give up our apartment in Vienna and move to Neulengbach in 1934, she came to visit us a few times. I remember that she always brought presents for us children. I can still see her in my mind's eye, a very slender brunette in a white silk dress with a red pattern. She was very nice to touch; she also

My father, aged 19, as a soldier

On Bisamberg with Frau Bender, 1933: Bruno, Helmut, Frau Bender, Therese and Theodor Schwebel

smelled wonderful, and unlike my mother, she used face powder and lipstick.

The apartment adjacent to ours belonged to Frau Bender, who had no children but an enormous soft bosom, my solace and refuge on more than one occasion. Very often we went walking with her, and I have kept a photo that shows all of us sitting on a tree trunk at Bisamberg, a favorite weekend destination for the people of Vienna.

It was a bit of an emotional drama for me when my brother started first grade and I had to stay home. Our elementary school was nearby, on the other side of Allerheiligenplatz, where Mama would sometimes buy us ice cream which the iceman, a fat Viennese with a big mustache, would neatly scoop onto cones with a wooden spatula. I'll never forget this ice-cream place. Even today, a dozen steps take me into a basement full of assorted goods that a nice Turk is trying to sell. It was always so pleasantly cool there that on summer days one did not want to leave. The Turk only sells packaged popsicles. Too bad. I had to go to Tichy's on Reumann-

Bruno, 4 years old, and Helmut, 6, (from left to right)

platz for a real ice-cream cone.

My mother was a good cook who always managed to conjure up a tasty meal, not counting a ragout made of calf's lung and known as "Beuschel," of course. But semolina pudding with lots of cinnamon: what wistful memories it stirs in me! On special occasions, she would spoil us with a dessert called "gebackene Mäuse," a kind of donut she served with raspberry juice. I also recall that, when we were little, we would spit in our soup and play "driftwood." But we also entertained ourselves with blocks, and an electric train still makes its rounds through my mind. Frequently, we were taken to a state-run agency to get ultraviolet radiation, which was thought to be healthy in those days. Sometimes my father would show up on a motorcycle he no doubt had borrowed from a colleague to take us for a ride back and forth on Handelskai, a street along the Danube without pedestrian traffic.

Sometimes we stayed on a farm where they rented rooms to vacationers, and I have a vague memory of my first encounter with the large yellow teeth of horses, with cows' udders, with teams of oxen, and with geese and how they pursued me with their dangerous-sounding trumpeting.

    The Prater is a part of Vienna's history. Its atmosphere today isn't much different than that of a *feria de pueblo* in Mexico, of an amusement park. We went there rarely because it was a good distance away, some of which I spent riding on Papa's shoulders. I really got a kick out of the Ferris wheel, the tunnel of horror, the electric cars, the slap-in-the-face man, a life-size figure, fat, with red cheeks who could be slapped with great bravado for a few groschen. (It is worth mentioning that this Austrian invention was later exported to Japan where frustrated employees could vent their anger on a mock-up of their boss.) But this symbol has meanwhile disappeared from the Prater; I, at any rate, failed to find it during my most recent sojourn in Vienna. Too bad. I had a strong desire to slap somebody without having to account for it. I firmly believe that he will be beaten to shreds by the frustrated guest workers and the jobless people who are looking for a little diversion here on their weekends.

    My father Theodor (Teddy) had a government job until February 1934, when the Socialist Uprising against the aggressive policies and the constant provocations of the Dollfuß administration ended in failure. We were relatively well off. From May 1922 until June 1934, my father worked for the Austrian Federation of Farm and Forestry Workers, among other obligations participating in the arbitration of labor conflicts. My father used to say, when he arrived in a village and could hear loud mooing, he could tell there were serious problems waiting for him because the striking workers refused to milk the cows.

    It became my great pleasure, and indeed a necessity so long as I was a child, to play in the garden or in the courtyard of our building. And as I look back, I see myself chasing a wooden hoop with a stick or wildly racing around on a treadle scooter. Mama watched over me from above. Very often we crossed the Danube on the Nordbahn Bridge to go for a walk on the flood plain along the other bank. It was always fun to cross the river. One could spit in the water, observe the passing ships, and listen to the shrieking sea gulls. Now there is a new bridge alongside the old one for the street car that goes into the districts on the other side of the river. There is also a modern shopping center nearby which, of course, didn't exist in Mama's time. It is run mostly by people from the East, from Turkey, Bulgaria, and Yugoslavia, who always seem to be bantering while they man the booths and stores here just as they do in the historic market area known as "Naschmarkt." They have adapted to Vienna by now and offer their wares with fluent recommendations, even though their native accents can still be clearly detected.

The meadows along the Danube exist to this day, of course, but they are full of little kiosks that cater to the people walking about. Reeds grow on parts of the shore. Even after I had arrived in Mexico, I dreamed sometimes that, pursued by Nazis, I was drifting toward Hungary fully submerged and getting air through a stalk of reed. There is a mosque now in the middle of these meadows. The open-air swimming pool on the river and several communal buildings are a heritage bequeathed by Vienna's Socialists. Farther in the distance are the Grinzing vineyards up Kahlenberg where Papa might buy us rock candy or a bottle of soda pop. Whenever we went to the meadows along the Danube, we were looking forward to the pickles that were sold there together with a glass of the famous mountain wellwater – presumably the purest water one can drink in any city. We flew our kites, laughed about our panicky fear of an approaching thunderstorm, or went to the Angelibad on the Old Danube in whose turbid waters my father, amid wild geese, swans, and ducks, gave me my first swimming lessons. Was it these experiences that made me later in Mexico use every river I crossed as an opportunity for a swim and cause me to admire Konrad Lorenz's experiences with the world of regional birds? Perhaps.

From 1911 until 1917, my father worked in the printing shop of the Rosenbaum brothers. He also took violin lessons for a few years and became a good musician. From 1929 until 1930, he studied violin at the Vienna Conservatory. I was told he played the background music for silent films. During the First World War – my father was drafted in February 1917 at the age of nineteen – he served in an Austro-Hungarian cavalry regiment on the Russian and Italian fronts.

I remember an anecdote I'd like to tell here: After the end of hostilities, my father was in a Russian prisoner-of-war camp (possibly in the Ukraine or in White Russia). It seems that he had permission to play at weddings and similar festivities in the area. Whenever I see Marc Chagall's *The Violin Player,* I am inevitably reminded of my father's privileged leaves while he was a prisoner of war. Once he was hailed as the great violinist from Vienna and a concert was arranged. Since he didn't have enough time to rehearse, he started to play simple polkas and waltzes, to the dismay of his frustrated audience of music lovers who left the hall one after the other. Papa always told this story cheerfully as a comic anecdote, but I am sure that at the time the situation was anything but funny for him. I know from my cousin Robert that Dora, his mother and my father's sister, and her husband, Samuel, went to Grzymalov, a village in Galicia where uncle Schwarz was born, on their wedding trip, and there they decided to take a train into revolutionary Russia where they looked for my father. A truly brave endeavor! The train was attacked by a notorious gang of Ukrainian nationalists whose leader was a certain Simon Petlyura. The bandits threw the Jews from the moving train and threatened my aunt that they would cut her finger off if she didn't surrender her wedding ring voluntarily. In defiance of all dangers, my aunt and uncle went from village to village in search of a violinist from Vienna. I find it hard to imagine that they actually found him, even though Robert is convinced of it because his mother stuck to this version of the story. They managed, at any rate, to return to Vienna, even though without a groschen in their pockets; they didn't have the fare for a streetcar.

My father was very depressed when he came back from the war and didn't know what to do with his life. He joined the Social Democratic Party as a Jew for whom a commitment to the Socialists was his only chance to be politically active. He was still working for the Party when he had to flee Austria. I'll never forgive myself for not having talked with him more about these and other stages of his life.

My brother and I attended the class for children at the Conservatory in Vienna. I was four or five years old. We took the streetcar, and since I became nauseated easily, we had to get off frequently and wait until I felt better, obviously arriving late for my lessons many times.

We had a piano at home, probably on loan, and a small violin

Theodor Schwebel in his office in the 1920s

for my brother. Papa saw to it that we did our homework, even though he was not very patient. But anyway, there was a recital at the Conservatory at the end of the course when I had to play a rather simple melody ("The Mill" by Franz Schubert) on the piano. I don't recall whether I lost my nerve toward the end or simply didn't know the piece well enough to continue. The fact is that I ran off the stage and, sobbing, sought refuge in my mother's arms. Everybody was laughing and trying to console me. Helmut did better with his selection for the violin. But this was the end of playing the piano for me until I started again thirty years later in the neighborhood of Santa María la Ribera in Mexico City, where I took a few lessons from an old gentleman and suffered through similar fears once more, but this time as a father, listening to my two sons, René and Daniel, at a children's recital. The anxiety, however, of choking up during a performance was to become a regular part of my career as an actor in Mexico.

My paternal grandfather was a watchmaker. He had a tiny shop in Sechhauser-Straße in the district of Rudolfsheim. Moritz Schwebel was born in the village of Czortkov in Galicia in present-day Poland on June 2, 1864. I was told that his father was a horse trader in this region of constant disturbances. He sold to Russians and Poles, bought or perhaps stole from them, just as circumstances may have required. So when someone these days tries to impress me with his family background, I won't hesitate to do him one better with my horse-thieving great-grandfather.

No one knows when my grandfather came to Vienna, but on September 4, 1889, he married Hermine (Hennie) Sara Kallenberg, born July 30, 1870, and thus joined the roughly thirty thousand families of Vienna's large Jewish community. My grandparents lived at 26 Grimmgasse, where my grandmother ran a small egg store. That is where my father was born on August 31, 1897, and that's probably also where his siblings started their lives: Helene, Dora, Josefine (Pepi), Oskar, and Rosi.

Opapa was a short, portly man who exuded much kindness. I've always kept a very vivid image of him, the way he wedged a magnifying glass against his nose while he was working on a watch. He was a cantor in the synagogue where my brother and I learned what little we would know about the Mosaic faith. Even though my father, being a socialist and atheist, showed minimal interest in things Jewish, he did take us, as I well remember, to Hebrew lessons – perhaps as a favor to Grandpa. I never in the years to come tried to broaden my education in this area. Grandfather died ten years later in the crematoria at Treblinka after they had picked him up together with other residents of a retirement home at Seegasse. That was on June 20, 1942. He was seventy-eight years old. My grandmother, Hennie Sara, was fortunate enough to die on November 26, 1936, from a brain embolism. Her daughters Pepi and Dora in Vienna looked after her until her death. My cousins Robert and Fredi Schwarz, seven and three years older than I, Aunt

Dora's and Uncle Schwarz's sons, told me that a physician tried to heal my grandmother by bleeding her, using Robert as his assistant. They also used electro-shock therapy to revive her paralyzed left side. She was buried in the Jewish Cemetery of Vienna. In 1961 my cousin Robert had the following inscription chiseled on her plain tombstone:

> Mourned by her husband
>
> In Memoriam
>
> Moses Schwebel
>
> Deported 1942

In Vienna we frequently visited the Schwarz family at their home in Missindorfstraße, at that time in the district of Hietzing. Aunt Dora was a petite woman with a full bosom who showed her fine character from the very beginning of the anti-Semitic excesses by confronting the constant provocations of some of the neighborhood women without ever losing her dignity. Uncle Schwarz, her calm, tight-lipped husband, owned a small clothing store. At home they played the piano and chess, and it was at their house that I was introduced to this game which I took up again later as a student in Mexico. My father admired my cousins, who were excellent students, and they in turn were very fond of him.

February 12, 1934, was a Monday. For some reason my father hadn't gone to work that day. We were walking down Engerthstraße. I remember very clearly that I was trying to stand balanced on a curb stone when we heard explosions close by. The fight between the Socialist *Schutzbund* (Protective League) and the Militia had started. We hurried home immediately. That night men I didn't know gathered in our apartment; there were fierce discussions and a lot of cigarettes were smoked. My brother and I had to stay in our room. There had been similar secret meetings during previous nights. The military suppressed the uprising of the Socialists quickly and brutally. Austria turned into a dictatorship, and all other political organizations were outlawed or disbanded. My father joined the long line of the unemployed.

There prevailed an atmosphere of great uncertainty. The population at large was getting ready for hard times. Would there be a general strike? People bought groceries and stored water but didn't stay indoors. We went with my father to inspect the heavily damaged Karl-Marx-Hof and other communal buildings. I tried to count the holes in the walls.

Then we were informed that Papa's younger brother, Oskar, had been arrested in St. Pölten and was being charged with high treason.

Chapter 2

NEULENGBACH

Shortly after the failure of the leftist uprising of February 12, 1934, the League of Farm and Forestry Workers was abolished and my father lost his job. This was the beginning of some hard years. Since we had to give up our apartment in Janecek-Hof, we moved into my grandfather's large house in Neulengbach, a small town some forty miles west of Vienna. On the advice of my father's younger brother, my uncle Oskar, Grandfather in 1919 had invested his meager savings in a piece of property that consisted of one rather run-down building and a huge garden with all kinds of fruit trees as well as walnut and hazelnut trees, covering an area of close to two and a half acres. Their intent had been to turn the harvest of pears and apples into cider, lease some of the rooms of the large house (known as "Haaghof") and use this income to pay off the mortgage.

Haaghof became the center of our Jewish family. Opapa had turned one of the rooms into a small store that opened onto a very busy road leading to a railroad viaduct. There were benches and tables in front of the store so that folks – many of them railroaders – could drink their bottle of beer, their glass of cider or a soda pop there. My cousin Robert tells that there was an old, toothless handyman by the name of Stolitzker, who did all the odd jobs for his meals and a few schillings. Robert remembers that the old guy would always complain to Aunt Pepi, who fixed his food, that there were never enough noodles in his soup.

After Opapa also Uncle Oskar moved into this town for good. Another room next to my grandfather's store was converted into Schwebel's "Community General Store" where my uncle sold all kinds of goods. A few years later, he moved his business closer to the center of town. I don't know how my father managed to provide for his family. The state paid him unemployment compensation. Often he went to Vienna, where he helped his relatives run their businesses, above all Uncle Max, Aunt Rosi's husband; she was Papa's youngest sister.

What is left of the partially renovated Haaghof still rises a little above the train tracks just a few minutes' walk from the Neulengbach station. Haaghof Lane formerly went past large storage buildings where sugar beets were kept for loading into boxcars and a sweetish smell of fermentation was all-pervasive. The Haaghof itself offered a view into the valley of the Tulln River and, from the back, into the center of town with its church, market place, school, the medieval castle from the 12th century and its surrounding forest of chestnut trees. I remember that every fall the path to the castle was covered with prickly, burst-open balls that revealed the large, shiny chestnuts. It is true: Neulengbach was and to this day is a pretty little town. "Welcome in Neulengbach, the Pearl of the Vienna Woods" reads the slogan on its poster. Today many Viennese yuppies have built their summer homes here. On weekends young couples frequent the "Alter Markt," a restaurant famous for its local mushroom-based delicacies. There are cultural events, or people visit the Egon Schiele Museum. The artist lived in the village for a few years, including a three-week stint in the local jail, where he finished a dozen watercolor paintings, after he had been reported to the police on a charge of indecency with minors. I often ask myself if my mother, who was ten years old at the time, remembered this incident or if she had been cautioned about it in school. Too bad it never crossed my mind to talk with her about it.

My grandparents lived in the Haaghof, also Aunt Rosi before she was married Max Wolfmann, my parents plus Helmut and me as well as Uncle Oskar with his children, Dita (Edith) and Herbert, both from his first marriage, to Marianne. Besides us, there were two or three renters, and a barber shop occupied one of the ground-floor rooms with a view of the village.

My mother never talked about it, but I don't think she ever felt at home there. She had no problems with Opapa – on the contrary. But there were frequent arguments with my grandmother, who was paralyzed on one side, used to giving orders, and hard to get along

Grandmother Hermine Schwebel,
end of 1920s

with. Mama had to fill in as her nurse. Omama probably never reconciled herself to the fact that my father had married a woman who wasn't Jewish.

My cousin Dita, Helmut and I went to school in Neulengbach. It was a twenty-minute walk into town which we spent playing. In the summer I sometimes walked barefoot but put my shoes back on in front of the school, where I finished first and second grade. I have fond memories of my teacher, Adelheid Weiss. Before classes we said the Lord's Prayer. I think I was aware of not being a Christian because one day as all the others were mumbling their "Our Father who art in Heaven," I got the idea of rocking back and forth, the way I had seen my relatives pray. Of course, I didn't do it out of religious conviction, but something had gotten into me to act differently. I am sure that made me the object of sneering glances, even though in the end I crossed myself like the other children.

In a side street off the town center, there existed a small prayer house which had been made available to the area's Jews and was opened only on holidays. Some eighty-five Jews lived in the vicinity, twenty of them in Neulengbach. I have no recollection of

Grandfather Moritz Schwebel,
about 1935

this prayer house though I am sure that I was taken there occasionally. During a recent visit I had a conversation with a friendly old gentleman who gave us a taxi ride to the Jewish cemetery a few miles outside of town. The relatively large number of graves took me by surprise, about seventy of them, none with visible traces of vandalism. These days just two or three Jewish families live in the area.

I very much liked to draw pictures. The red, richly decorated heart I painted for my mother every year was always received with many kisses. Once I sketched a tree with hanging and broken-off branches, which met with praise from Miss Weiss. My weakness was gymnastics. I never managed to pull myself up a rope even by an inch, and it took much sweat and toil to turn head-over-heels or to do the obligatory jumps over the pommel horse. During my first two years in elementary school, I had grades of "excellent" in all subjects, even in gym! Even today, I add and multiply in German, mumble the German alphabet when I use a dictionary, and still know how to write in German script.

When I visited Neulengbach in the 1970s, I went to the school and looked into my old classroom. Wistful and curious, I tried to recognize myself in one of the boys who looked the way I did seventy years ago. Had I been as wellbehaved as he? I noticed their orderliness. All children were quiet and raised their hands for permission to speak. My spontaneous reaction was to think of the relaxed atmosphere at the Montessori school my sons attended in Mexico. I got a better understanding of how the principle of education for conformity works, and I was reminded of the word Einstein coined for "blind obedience" (*Kadavergehorsam*) to define his experiences in German schools. Indeed, "cadavers" don't rebel.

On our daily walk home from school, we passed a plague column, a reminder of the plague year of 1680. Sometimes we watched a game of soccer or rummaged around what was left of a farmstead that we had watched from the Haaghof as it burned to the ground. On Sundays Papa would occasionally take us to the Tulln, which at that time carried more water than it does now. At one place there was built a temporary dam out of boards to create a swimming hole. The kids from town would dive in head first and I made my first belly-flops, anxiously watched by my father. I am sure that these adventures, no less than my first experiences in the Old Danube in Vienna, nourished my passion for rivers, springs, and ponds.

It's about an hour's walk across open country to Haspel Forest. In the center of it, in a particularly dense stand of trees, there was a deep, overgrown ditch. It is said that the people from Neulengbach hid there during the Turkish siege of Vienna in 1683, which also affected the area around here. They were discovered and all of them were massacred when a crowing rooster alerted the enemy. I still know that this place made me imagine all kinds of frightful things: scimitars decapitating people and boys (like me) being turned into eunuchs.

Grandfather, always on an even keel and full of love, unthinkable without his pipe and his cane, was the axis around which our life turned. He had a good sense of humor, which my father inherited from him, and he was always surrounded by us, his grandchildren, who fought over who would be allowed to sit on his knees. They tell me that around 1940, hiking with a cane, he tried to cross the Swiss border – like someone who was just taking a stroll out into the countryside.

There were many more opportunities for playing during our vacations, when the cousins from Vienna arrived: Fredi, small but very agile in body and mind (he could even do handstands and turn a cartwheel); his older brother Robert, serious and intellectual; chubby Erika, dear and clumsy; Reni, almost grownup, the oldest one among us; Lizzi, fragile and feminine, even at the age of five or six; Aunt Toni's children; Aunt Klara's kids, Paula and her little sister Lisa, Aunt Dobbe's daughter, and a few more cousins on grandmother's side. I have a photo that shows the assembled Schwebel-Kallenberg clan on a lawn at the Haaghof: a large group of relatives who clearly are enjoying their lives, dear and affectionate folk. Many of them did not survive the Holocaust. But I remember only a few of those who are shown in the picture. My cousin Fredi maintains that on one occasion he counted seventy-two family members. And he recalls that Opapa would sometimes go into Vienna with a sack full of fruit for his grandchildren, windfalls from the orchard that one could use only for making jam.

For us children, the Haaghof was a giant playground for adventurous games. The large, untended garden, its weeds nearly as tall as I, was an ideal place to play hide-and-seek. "Behind me, before me, left, right, no fair," was what the seeker would usually holler. One challenge among the boys was to climb the nut trees at the edge of the garden and pee down from the highest branches. We chased the goats, explored a little creek along the boundary line of the property, or rummaged around the attic, where fruit and vegetables were stored. But we were not allowed in the basement, where grandfather had his fruit press and where the pear cider and beer he sold in his store were kept cool.

We put on shows, acting like cops and robbers, or, inspired by Karl May's stories, we changed into cowboys and Indians. We fought over who would play the heroes of these tales. The big kids claimed the roles of Old Surehand, Old Shatterhand, or the noble redskin Winnetou while I usually was left with being one of their sidekicks. In the evening we had permission to watch the grownups play cards; we also helped grandfather get rid of his warts by tying them off with a piece of thread, pulled out his white hairs, which even earned us a groschen per hair, or waited in our bedrooms, which had a direct view of the tracks, for the train from Vienna, the

The Schwebel-Kallenberg family in the garden of the Haaghof, 1929. In the buggy on the right: Bruno

"fire train," as we called it. Its locomotive seemed to be shrouded in flames. When it thundered past us, at a distance of just a few yards, the whole Haaghof shook and our joy knew no end.

We had a dog called Murli and a cat whose territory included the Haaghof and its environs. I remember that Adidin Loban Sudai – yes, for whatever reason, that's the name we had given her – surprised us children with how exceptionally often she had kittens.

The rooms of the house were arranged around a courtyard in whose center a mighty linden tree spread its branches over a table and benches where we sometimes would eat. From there a trail led to the chicken coop and the well and elderberry bushes with white blossoms and then berries that the birds considered special delicacies. The well was forbidden terrain for the little ones, myself included. Mulberry bushes and creepers grew along the walls of the building. We had currant shrubs, the fruit of which Mama boiled to make jelly. At one end of the courtyard was a vegetable garden and behind it stood low trees that bore big juicy pears, Kaiserbirnen. In the spring the area was often infested with June bugs. We tied the little beasties down with a length of thread and used these living airplanes to engage in all sorts of aerobatic competitions.

At the start of spring, the first snowdrops came up on the

Haaghof in 1954, with a part of Uncle Oskar's store

meadows and left little funnels in the snow as they grew taller. Later on, we could discover the true violets and their magnificent fragrance in moist and shady places where they would sometimes hide among the taller but scentless dogtooth violets. Whenever I listen to Vivaldi's *Four Seasons*, "Summer" invariably abducts me to the fields near Neulengbach. The Allegro conjures up a gathering thunderstorm and during the cello cadenzas, I sleepwalk the meadows in search of a four-leaf clover that will bring me luck. We picked wild strawberries and made necklaces from dandelion stems. The grain fields filled up with red poppies, marsh marigolds, and wild daisies, my mother's favorite flowers. Often we also went looking for mushrooms, especially parasol mushrooms, which are a special treat when sautéed with breadcrumbs. The woods took us in with a pleasant coolness, with the aroma of damp soil and rotting plants. There was always a deep silence, accompanied only by the quiet murmur of the wind swaying the mighty tops of pine trees and beeches or by a distant cuckoo calling.

In April 1938, my grandfather had to register his property with the Austrian Nazi authorities in a "Roster of Jewish Assets," which assessed the lot and buildings at fourteen thousand marks. In September 1939, he was forced to sell it considerably below market value. There is every indication that the buyer, a certain Otto Bartosik, had to pay off no more than an existing mortgage before he took possession of the Haaghof. My grandfather was interned in a Jewish retirement home to which his mother, over ninety years old, had also been transferred. These are the facts about the Haaghof. There are only a few survivors who can testify to its emotional value.

I have always wanted to visit the Haaghof in the company of my surviving cousins to reminisce with them about those years: Reni, Aunt Helene's daughter, who lives in Israel; Lizzi, the daughter of Rosi and Max, who miraculously saved herself from being deported from the terrible Camp Drancy near Paris and at this time lives in Val d'Or in northern Canada; Robert and Fredi who settled in the United States; Dita and Herbert who found a new home in Mexico; as well as my brother Helmut and I, who also put down roots in Mexico.

During one of my visits, I spoke about the emigration of my family with a woman who had been a renter at the Haaghof and who remembered me as a child. Her answer was that of many Austrians when they are confronted with the Holocaust: What a hard time they had had! The Russians had been veritable monsters, the women had to hide to escape being raped, the shock troops confiscated everybody's watches, and German howitzers were shooting at the Russians across the Haaghof.

When in September 2000 I walked by the Haaghof with my wife, Joan, the building had a new roof. The garden had been sub-divided, and new houses were being built on some of the lots. In the center of the courtyard, where our beloved linden tree had stood, a few people – were they perhaps relatives of that Herr Bartosik? – were having their lunch, chatting and paying no attention to the stranger who, tears in his eyes, couldn't decide if he should introduce himself and ask for permission to look around. I wanted to avoid having my emotions offended by the trivial remarks of some ignoramus. I did not want to have to explain the tears I couldn't hold back. My memory of that large family coming together at the Haaghof in Neulengbach – I wanted to keep it free of shadows.

Chapter 3

NEULENGBACH IN THE 1920s

In 1420, two Jews were burned at the stake in Enns after they had confessed under torture to having desecrated a sacramental wafer. The banishment of the Jewish community from Vienna followed the year after, leading to the death of several thousand people by fire. Anti-Semitism has been firmly rooted in Austria ever since – "deep in the Austrian soul," as people say. This brought about the destruction of one-third of the 200,000 Jews living in this country before the Nazi era.

But for all that, it was an accepted and partially even cherished fact, especially during the reign of Emperor Francis Joseph, that the Jews of Vienna, that "Gateway to the East," lived in peace with other ethnic minorities (people from the Caucasus, Hungarians, Slavs, Poles, Turks) and religious groups (Christians, Muslims). It is well-known that Jews (Arnold Schönberg, Gustav Mahler, Franz Werfel, Stefan Zweig, Alfred Adler, Arthur Schnitzler, Sigmund Freud, Otto Bauer, Max Adler, to name but a few) made extremely significant contributions to the city's political and cultural life.

Anti-Semitism in Neulengbach was no different than anti-Semitism in the rest of the country. One example of this is the fact that in the 12th century a gate was built on the main street to separate the market place from the Jewish quarter in which a number of merchant families lived. It is known that at a later time signs were posted saying "For good Christians only," especially in apartments that were rented to summer vacationers, and plays were performed that fomented the hatred of Jews.

For these reasons, the presence of the Schwebel family and above all the activities of the brothers Teddy and Oskar during the

Therese and Theodor Schwebel at the Haaghof, 1924

1920s were unusual occurrences which the historian Robert Streibel has described in his book *February in the Backwoods* (1994).

Uncle Oskar was the first Schwebel to become active in and around Neulengbach, at that time a town of about one thousand. It is possible that this endeavor resulted from his work in behalf of the Social Democratic Party, in which he held an important position. This party enabled Jews to engage in political activities, a fact that was to assume great significance. The rightist Christian opposition was, of course, not suitable for the political ambitions of the Jews. Streibel points out in his book that both my uncle and my father were pioneers of the workers' movement in the region around Neulengbach.

It was a successful strategy of the Party to have its functionaries organize cultural as well as political events. The enthusiasm with which the Schwebel brothers fostered the educational life of the region no doubt came from a personal artistic quest. Their work was supported by their wives, non-Jewish women from the area. In 1924 Uncle Oskar married Marianne Stocker, and my father wed Therese (Reni) Hössinger, my mother. So far as I know, these marriages helped most of the time to shield the Schwebel clan from

Wedding picture of my parents, 1924

open hostility. My mother was the youngest daughter and also the prettiest of the Hössingers. When my father met her, she was working for Dr. Ernst Taussig, a Jewish lawyer in Neulengbach who survived the Nazi era. She stayed with him until 1925. She and her sister-in-law, Marianne, participated actively and enthusiastically in the cultural events. Both had beautiful voices, and my father as well as my uncle played the violin, Father serving as the conductor and his brother as the artistic director of their performances. Together with other friends from the area they also started a theater group, "Thea."

I have saved a number of playbills from that time. One of the shows was the musical comedy *Hannerl*, by Willner and Reichert, in which Marianne, along with twenty other amateur actors, had a part. Other plays were *On Orders from the Duchess*, *The Dance into Happiness* and *The Lucky Girl*; the program also included operettas, readings, violin duos played by the Schwebel brothers, choir concerts, and poetry evenings. Aside from these performances, my father conducted the band of the town's Socialist Protective League. Contemporary historians and political scientists who specialize in this period attest that the Schwebels brought a touch of culture to Neulengbach and the neighboring communities during the 1920s.

Our Uncle Oskar was politically very active in this region as a leader of the social-democratic movement. He coordinated the

The Schwebel brothers, Oskar and Teddy, in Neulengbach, 1920s

construction of a workers' home and wrote for and distributed the socialist weekly newspaper, *Volkswacht*, which was published from 1918 until 1934. When a general strike was called in Vienna on February 12, 1934, his activities were centered in St. Pölten. By chance, it was he who took the call informing them that the Socialist Uprising in Vienna had started, information he passed on, of course. For that, he was charged with high treason and put on trial. It is remarkable that he acted as his own defense attorney. He was incarcerated in St. Pölten for six months. His family was deeply worried. He divorced Marianne after his release; his children, Dita and Herbert, stayed with him. A short time later he married Anni Wolf, who had a daughter, and they started a new life in Wetzlas near Zwettl in the Waldviertel of Lower Austria, where my cousin Alfons was born.

My father's political activities are not quite as well remembered. I never found the right occasion to talk to him about this, which I now regret. No doubt they were concentrated in Vienna where he had moved with my mother in the summer of 1926.

There were probably many "Schwebel brothers" during that dramatic and confused time in European history. From our perspective today, my father's contribution in support of the organized working class, its long road from exploitation to active resistance and the consolidation of its rights during the 1920s, may have been insignificant. But I am proud of his work even though it is little known. I am not sure to what degree my respect for his activities has influenced my own political thinking. It is a fact, though, that the principles of Social Democracy are deeply rooted in me and form the foundation of my political convictions, even as these principles are being displaced by a global capitalism that denies billions of people the chance for economic progress.

Theatersektion des sozialdem. Bildungs-Ausschusses
Neulengbach-Tausendblum.

PROGRAMM

»Hannerl«

Singspiel in 3 Akten von Dr. A. M. Willner und Heinz Reichert.
Musik von Franz Schubert, f. d. Bühne bearbeitet von Prof. E. Lafite.

Regie: Oskar Schwebel.   Dirigent: Theodor Schwebel.

Personen:

Baron Schober, Hofrat	Josef Wösendorfer
Johanna, dessen Frau	Hermine Wachter
Hannerl ⎫	Marianne Schwebel
Franz ⎬ beider Kinder	Anton Nostok
Kl. Georg ⎭	Kl. Kurt Jellinek
Christian Tschöll	Fritz Schiller a. G.
Baron Hans von Gumpenberg	Oskar Schwebel
Frau Barbara Stumpf	Leopoldine Skokan
Helene, deren Tochter	Hermine Salmutter
Gräfin Clementine Droszy, Stiftsdame	Käthe Nickmann
Komtesse Aranka, deren Nichte	Grete Umstätter
Polizeirat Nowotny	Fritz Cernuschek
Brucker, Gesangslehrer	Leopold Salmutter
Bruneder	Ferdinand Skokan
Niedinger ⎫	Leopold Salmutter
Kupelwieser ⎬ Studenten	Franz Fuß
Haslinger ⎭	Josef Wösendorfer
Obermüller	Willy Tschebaum
Mali, Mädchen bei Schober	Anna Fiala
Frau Dussek	Emilie Schuster
Frau Zillinger	Leopoldine Skokan

Ort der Handlung: 1. Akt: Wohnzimmer bei Baron Schober.
2. Akt: Vorraum eines Wiener Ballsaales.
3. Akt: Salon bei Baron Schober.

Spielt im Jahre 1849 in Wien.

Nach dem 1. und 2. Akt größere Pause.

Zuspätkommende finden erst nach dem 1. Akt Einlaß.

Programm: K 1000.

Playbill, 1925

Uncle Oskar and Hans Hössinger (Mama's younger brother) in front of his store in Neulengbach, mid-1920s

Chapter 4

THE HÖSSINGERS

The telephone directories for Neulengbach and surrounding towns all the way to St. Pölten list many people named Hössinger. Probably a number of them are descendants of my great-grandfather Franz Hössinger and thus are relatives of mine.

I don't know how many sons my great-grandfather and his wife, Anna Rankl, had. It must have been quite a few, as was customary in the 1850s. My grandfather Joseph was one of them. He was born in 1869 and married Maria Unterreiter in the mid-1890s. They had ten children, among them my mother, who joined them on March 3, 1902. One day my artistic love of trees made me draw the Hössinger family tree as far back as my great-great-grandparents. So if one of my descendants should run into a Wiedenhofer, Rankl, Deltenweitz, Laimeraner, or Zinsmayr, he can introduce himself as a distant relative. And if he's interested in genetics and math, he could calculate the number of genes they have in common.

My Catholic grandparents lived in a few rooms of a modest house near the Neulengbach station and a few minutes away from the Haaghof where my Jewish grandparents on my father's side lived. Even with the short distance between their houses, I doubt that they ever went to visit. I'm not even sure that they knew each other, although my father socialized with them. My mother did often take us there for a visit, but all I remember are simple furnishings, sepia-colored photographs, a small, sprightly grandmother, and a strong old-folks smell. We were forbidden to roam about the neighborhood on account of a nearby clay pit where many a child had come to grief.

At Christmastime all the Hössingers gathered round the old people, who had a Christmas tree with home-baked cookies. I am

Grandmother Maria and Grandfather Joseph Hössinger

told that I had wanted to know at one time why my Jewish grandparents didn't decorate a "Jewmas" tree. As tradition demanded, old St. Nicholas, a rather sinister figure quite unlike his jovial descendant, Santa Claus, gave good boys like me a few sweets. The bad kids were taken away by Krampus, a devil completely dressed in red, who carried them off in a sack he slung over his shoulder.

There was a beer garden across from the station with tables and benches under chestnut trees where grandfather had a place reserved for him alone. He was a retired railroader, kindly and unassuming. I felt very good in his company, as he apparently did in mine, since I only remember him smiling. He died in 1936. I won't forget the day when we at the Haaghof received the news of his death, and Mama started to cry. I also had tears in my eyes though I don't know whether I cried because everybody else did or because I had to go to the funeral or because I realized that I would never see Grandfather again. My grandmother, Maria, whom I barely remember, died at the end of 1941 as we were desperately trying to save our lives by escaping from Gestapo-infiltrated Vichy France. A few years ago, I heard that she and other Hössingers could never understand why my mother had married a Jew and

My Aunts Paula and Anni, 1954

much less why she had followed him abroad with her children. Perhaps they knew nothing about the Nuremberg Laws of September 15, 1935, and their enforcement in Austria after the Annexation, which meant that all Jews had to be registered and then were excluded from public life. According to these laws, my brother and I would have been deported and perhaps murdered.

During my visit to Neulengbach in September 2000, I found Opapa's beer garden closed, tables and benches chained together, the clay pit gone. My grandparents' house wasn't easy to recognize in the midst of a new housing development. It had been renovated. A brown child, probably an immigrant's son, was looking at me suspiciously through a closed window with aluminum frames. I am sure he was wondering what I was doing there. Would I have played with him as a little boy? There were no brown children in my school.

Uncle Hans, my mother's youngest brother, was a sportsman and had, as many Hössingers do, myself included, a high forehead and a tendency to grow bald. He helped out in my Jewish grandfather's store in the Haaghof and later married Aunt Hanni who charms everyone without fail the moment they see her picture in my album of family photographs. She was my mother's best friend during her time in Neulengbach. Uncle Hans lived in a small house next to the Haaghof. He was the artist of the Hössinger clan. I liked visiting him at home best of all and watching him paint water colors of landscapes and of animals. Some of them now hang in my living room, among them a drawing, "House near Zakopane," he made as a German soldier during the war. He was killed on the Russian front in February 1945.

Aunt Paula was six years older than my mother. She and her husband, Hans Groll, were members of the socialist movement around Neulengbach during the 1920s. I loved Aunt Paula, who would embrace me with the affection of childless aunts whenever we came to see her in her little house outside of Tausendblum. And then she would cook me one of my favorite meals or give me pieces of fruit from her orchard.

My mother had a very cordial relationship with her sister Anni, who was small but bighearted. She was married to Rudolf Teichmann, also a railroader, a jovial man of whom I have only the best of recollections. They lived in Purkersdorf on the main road that connects Vienna with western Austria. During our frequent visits, my aunt always spoiled us with desserts or with a special bacon sandwich and tea. My brother and I played with Kurt, who was our age. He was small and cross-eyed. We usually did jigsaw puzzles or competed naming the makes of cars that were passing through town. Rudi, the older son, I barely remember. He was a Nazisympathizer. After the Annexation, he went to Germany, worked in an aircraft plant, was trained as a Luftwaffe pilot, and was shot down on the Russian front.

During my first trip to Austria in 1954, with my first wife, Mati, I met Kurt's daughters, Helga and Herta, when they were young girls. I was driving a brand-new Citroën I had rented in Paris. As we were going for a ride up and down the streets in town, the girls were greatly worried that the tires might get dirty from the numerous horse apples.

I unpack this anecdote at every suitable occasion, for example, the last time I visited these relatives (who are grandmothers now) and their families and the youngest generation of Grandpa Hössingers's descendants. But I make no attempt to bring old dramas back to life even though, as always, I pay careful attention to indications of anti-Semitism. We speak about Austria's great prosperity and agree that the absence of horse apples from the neighborhood streets and roads is a sure sign of it. The possible objection some of them may still harbor against this somewhat distant Jewish relative gives way to the curiosity and the desire to get to know me better. I, for my part, try to discover family characteristics in their facial features and gestures, but the only obvious signs are, and continue to be, the Hössingers' high forehead and a mutual appreciation of Wiener schnitzels and beer.

My cousin Meli, the daughter of Aunt Mitzi, Mama's oldest sister, married Karl Schlatzer, a simple, hard-working man. They saved enough money to buy a modest house in Furth near Neulengbach; they also own a well-tended vegetable garden and a few fruit trees which, when they bloom, make me wish I could paint like Vincent van Gogh. We are always welcome there. When my parents went back to Austria for a visit, the Schlatzers put them up. But on every return, my father was left with a painful emptiness because his whole family was dead, and he had lost nearly all contacts with his fellow party members.

In a high school in Korneuburg near Vienna, I felt renewed hope that Austria's young generation may have a less racist mentality than their ancestors. During my visit to Vienna in March 2000, one of the teachers invited me to talk to her students about my experiences with Nazism and about our emigration. I was surprised by the impeccable behavior of these young people and by the interest they showed in this topic, even though their knowledge of it was slight. It was easy to answer their main question, why I didn't return after the war, with the counter-question "For what reason?" and to point out that as a seventeen-year-old I had put down roots in Mexico. I had some difficulty only with explaining why Juárez had had the Hapsburg Emperor Maximilian executed by a firing squad.

I was also surprised by the lively interest the young generation took in the exhibit of *The Crimes of the Wehrmacht* when I saw it during my sojourn in Vienna and then read a report in the newspaper *Der Standard* about the reactions of the people who had also gone to see it. I thought the attitude of a group of young people was remarkable when they heard an old woman's comment that the clashes in Vienna during the 1930s were understandable since the city had been so full of Jews.

Also the work of organizations like the study-and-action group *Youth against Violence and Racism,* whose director I met in Graz, make me feel hopeful.

Chapter 5

PURKERSDORF

Purkersdorf lies on the outskirts of Vienna and is surrounded by woods, thanks to Herr Schöffel. On weekends tourists hike up Schöffelstein or Rudolfshöhe to enjoy the panoramic view and then to recuperate from their exertions in one of the numerous inns. Whenever I come across the name of Josef Schöffel, a naturalist who fought against the massive clear-cutting in the Vienna Woods that was done to pay the debts accrued in connection with the War of 1866, I can't help being reminded of the laxly controlled way the jungles of Chiapas and Tabasco and the woods of Durango are being deforested.

It was impractical for Father to be making these constant trips back and forth between Vienna and Neulengbach, which is the reason, I think, we moved to Purkersdorf in 1936. My father could do the ten miles into the city by bicycle. Together with my cousin Fredi, he was to be retrained as a typewriter repairman. Fredi soon gave up. But my father seemed to have applied what he had learned in the course he took, although I don't know if the oil he had on his hands at the end of the day came from the typewriters or from his bicycle.

First we lived in the addition to a house that exists to this day, 32 Bahnhofstraße, a few paces past the village station of Unter-Purkersdorf. It was a street with mighty trees, continuing into the center of town past a small square with a monument in honor of those who had died in the Great War. There is a hotel now where the monument once stood, patriotism having been replaced by the profit motive. A table with benches and a swing had been added to the little courtyard behind the house and from there a footpath led down to a creek, the Wien, that empties into the Danube.

There was a trail along this creek where we would sometimes take a Sunday walk. On one of these walks, I found a pocket knife and, a little later that same day, two coins. These finds left a lasting impression on me. I often dream of this path by the creek, my lucky trail. During my visit in 1997, I retraced my steps and kept my eyes close to the ground, hoping I might again find something. But I discovered only some passers-by, who sized me up with suspicion, and in the distance, a doe turning tail.

The old house where Aunt Anni, Uncle Rudolf, and my cousins Kurt and Rudi lived was just around the corner. Their two-room apartment was on the ground floor; their windows looked out on to Main Street. I always see this house with Uncle Rudolf sitting by the window and watching traffic. When television appeared in the fifties, he vacated his customary place. The house stood close to the forest which started a few yards behind the small gardens of the tenants. Deer came down the slope in winter to feed on the vegetable scraps Aunt Anni left out for them.

Across from the first train stop of the town (Purkersdorf-Sanitarium) was a hospital, famous for its architecture and furnishings after designs by Josef Hoffmann. Mama worked there in maintenance. On the grounds of the hospital stood a house in which a Jewish family with a sickly boy lived. His name was Georg, and he never had anyone to play with. We sometimes went to see him and spent long hours with his collection of tin soldiers. The cannons had a carriage with a spring that could fire off peas. I think this family tried to emigrate to the United States since my brother remembers that we were to resume our games in San Francisco. I hope they managed to get out. I assume that my mother was given money or perhaps also groceries for our playing with Georg.

Most of the housewives did their laundry in a wooden tub. My brother got the idea that we should use one of these tubs for a trip all the way to Vienna. We took some extra boards and tar to refit an old unused wash tub, but our boat leaked, and so our adventure stayed within the confines of the imagination.

In a neighboring house lived a girl my age with whom I "played doctor" under the protection of a small bridge until we were caught by surprise. Even though we were severely scolded, the experience left no traces in my psyche. At least so I believe. Father's family hardly ever came to see us. But I do remember quite well a visit from Aunt Rosi, Uncle Max, and my cousin Lizzi who was about four years younger than I. While we were playing, I must have done something very inappropriate because there was general snickering and afterward we were no longer allowed to use the swing.

The school was in the center of town, between the train tracks and Main Street. I barely remember our third-grade teacher, a Herr Endl. I had a very good report card, but not in gym. My teacher in fourth grade was Herr Atzinger, a person very popular with everyone according to some of my relatives on my mother's side. I finished the first half of fourth grade in July 1938, three months after the Annexation. I was given a grade of "very good" in all subjects, including Religion, even though I was registered as a Jew. A mistake? Perhaps a gesture by Herr Atzinger? Could be. This was the end of my schooling in Austria, which had been renamed Ostmark, the Eastern March.

My mother attached pieces of cloth to the ceiling of our room in order to dry the sliced mushrooms we had gathered in the surrounding woods. That was one of our frequent pleasures. All we had to do was go to the nearby station, cross the tracks on a wooden bridge that led to the platforms, and climb the slope on the other side. And there we were: in the Vienna Woods. We were like everyone else, we had our secret spots which we reached in roundabout ways to confuse potential spies. A few years earlier, we might have run into Sigmund Freud, also an enthusiastic mushroom gatherer, in this area. As I write this, I permit myself the chutzpah of phantasizing that I am having an espresso with Freud in his favorite Café Landtmann while we analyze our mutual passion. I have kept this fondness for mushrooms ever since. In Mexico I avidly looked for egg mushrooms or the edible boletus in the forest of Tlalpan or Avándaro, near El Chico it was morels, and in Tepoztlán, underneath rotting tree trunks, it was oyster mushrooms.

In the center of town was a movie theater. I remember the announcement for *The Cabinet of Dr. Caligari,* a German classic. Movies were too expensive for us, however. But somehow we did hear about the achievements of the black athlete, Jesse Owens, at the Olympic Games in Berlin, about his world record in the 100-

meter dash and his kick-style broad jumps. The village also had a public library where I first encountered the stories of Karl May and other "western" tales. There was not one boy who wasn't enthusiastic about their heroes. My greatest pleasure was drawing galloping horses that I copied from illustrated books. The library is still there today. One sees many boys with long hair and wearing dirty sneakers but one can be sure that they still read the same books we read sixty years ago and just as passionately. A few paces down the street was the office where the jobless were paid their unemployment compensation. I still see my father standing in line with his bicycle. The office exists to this day but there are no lines. They disappeared with the arrival of general prosperity.

After some time, my parents rented an apartment on the second floor of a house at the edge of town. It was a pretty building with four apartments at 22 Rechenfeldstraße. It was to be our last address in Austria. The street was quiet and wide, part of a sparsely populated neighborhood. At the end of the street was a bowling alley next to an inn with a tap room. Occasionally we earned a few groschen from the bowlers for lining up their pins. In winter we got our sleds out and coasted down a fairly steep clearing, which has now been made into a parking lot for weekenders. Nowadays much of the area is taken up by a sports center near the throughway from Vienna to western Austria. When you ask for information, people tend to answer in an unfriendly and suspicious tone of voice.

On one of my trips, I was changing the film in my camera on the trunk lid of a parked car. Right away the owner came running out of a store. He snapped at me, saying I could have scratched the paint, and got into his car. Perhaps he was right, but I thought his reaction was excessive and I didn't want to leave it at that, so I knocked on his side window, which the fellow rolled down, but the only thing I could think of at that moment was to ask: "Do you speak English?"

"Naa!" he answered in his broad accent.

"Naa?, well then . . . ," I replied.

Suddenly all the cuss words we had hurled at each other as youngsters and that I hadn't used for sixty years came back to me, especially those involving "ass kissing" and its numerous variations.

They bubbled out of me in an interminable stream of words I threw at him in purest Viennese. I'll never forget the expression on his face before he shifted into reverse and stepped on the gas.

Our life before the Annexation was quiet, even though my father was very tense, I am sure on account of what was going on in Germany. He frequently went to Vienna. Sometimes it was days before he returned. On Sundays we went on hikes through the surrounding countryside. Papa taught us how to ride a bicycle, and sometimes we took the train to Neulengbach to see Grandfather and Uncle Oskar and his family. In summer we picked wild raspberries and splashed in the nearby creek. I remember a neighbor who showed us how to catch trout with our bare hands between the water plants along the bank. My brother was more adventurous than I. Once he nearly broke his neck falling off a tree in a neighbor's garden.

I remember that my father was always taciturn and that my mother worked in the kitchen silently. There was little laughter. We saw hard times coming.

German troops occupied Austria on March 12, 1938. On their way to Vienna, they also came though Purkersdorf. It was a Saturday, school classes had been dismissed. Main Street was near our house and passed through a tunnel under the train tracks. The convoys of military vehicles and tanks held an irresistible attraction for a nine-year-old boy. Together with my brother and other neighborhood boys, I watched the military engineers as they constructed a detour at the edge of town around the tunnel, which was too low for some of the vehicles. That day I got home late. My father was very worried and beside himself. He gave me a thrashing, the first and only time in my life. Two days later there was a rumor that Hitler would be coming through by train on his way to Vienna. It was close to noon and there were still no classes. Even though the train went by very fast, we children thought we had seen Hitler waving from his window. I was aware that I had done something my father would not have approved of.

The attraction of all these happenings for me was obvious and understandable. The troops set up a public soup kitchen in town where they served stew – free of charge. I went there more than once without telling my parents. From one day to the next, huge red flags with a swastika were flying everywhere. The German national anthem, "Deutschland, Deutschland, über alles . . ." and the Horst-Wessel-Song ("Raise the flag, our columns in tight formation") were played incessantly from schools and public buildings. This march especially impressed itself on my childlike memory for the rest of my life. Did I comprehend the true meaning of Chancellor Schuschnigg's national referendum of March 13 to vote for an independent, social and Christian, German, and united Austria? Certainly not. As little as I was able to understand fully why my parents were horrified at the events everyone else was welcoming enthusiastically.

During the first weeks, the behavior of the Viennese Nazis was worse than that of their comrades in Germany. In a few days, close to 80,000 non-sympathizers were arrested, and the horrible outrages committed against the Jews were known very well all over the world, a silent world that had been intimidated by Hitler's transgressions. Mexico, through its left-wing government under Lázaro Cárdenas, was the only country that instructed its ambassador to the League of Nations, Don Isidro Fabela, to protest against the Annexation.

We were not directly affected by the anti-Semitic violence in Purkersdorf, probably because we didn't look Jewish – a Hössinger inheritance – and my father was relatively unknown in public. But many of the approximately seventy Jews who lived in Purkersdorf at that time had to suffer terrible abuse. I certainly was very afraid, not on account of any particular incident at the outset, but after the first expressions of hatred in town, I was scared for quite specific and ever increasing reasons. For all that, my brother and I kept going to school where classes started with the Hitlersalute and where we were sometimes called nasty names like "filthy Yid" or "Jew, Jew, spit in your shoe." Once a group of schoolboys threw stones at us. We had to jump over the barriers at the train crossing and were able to escape. Starting in August, we were barred from attending classes. I would have been in fifth grade. Since we were not allowed to go to school, we had to help Mama with all the little chores and tend the vegetable garden. Another task was to go into the forest and gather firewood for the kitchen. There wasn't much of it left because everybody else was doing what we did. We took a long pole with hooks that we always hid well and broke dry branches off the trees. To be able to carry what we had collected, we would tie the sticks into two bundles that formed the letter V and lift the open end over our shoulders. That way we could drag the branches out. Then we had to chop the wood, stack it up behind the house, and protect it from the rain and snow.

Sometimes I had a fantasy that I could hide from the persecutions in the woods. I thought they wouldn't find me in the top of a tree or in a ditch covered with dry leaves.

One day I had an accident. I was swinging on the iron gate that opened out into the front yard, the gate closed on my arm and trapped me – the scar is still there. I was bleeding from a deep cut above my wrist, which I was stupid enough to try to hide from my mother. When Papa came home, he immediately took me to Vienna by train. The situation was so urgent that we were forced to go to a German military hospital. It seems they didn't ask many questions, perhaps to make a good impression as friends of the Austrian people. How would they have reacted to my being circumcised? I was lucky not to have to pull down my underpants. I'm sure Papa was very concerned. I was given a local anesthetic and a good number of stitches. I remember that it hurt a lot. After the surgery, the doctor praised me and said I'd make a great member of the Hitler Youth.

I doubt that my father, on account of his political past, continued to receive his unemployment compensation. Paradoxically, he had friends among the National Socialists. They were former colleagues whose political convictions had made them switch to the ranks of the Nazi Party, which accepted them. One of them – I regret not knowing his name – saved my father's life and a few weeks later ours as well.

On November 7, 1938, the German-Polish Jew Herschel Grynszpan entered the German Embassy in Paris and shot the legation secretary, Ernst vom Rath, two days later. The Nazi leaders used this assassination to start the organized pogroms known to history as *Kristallnacht* (the Night of Broken Glass). All Jewish institutions were damaged or destroyed. Synagogues, books and documents were burned. The arrests and indignities inflicted on human beings had no end. These activities were the beginning of the Holocaust.

National Socialists, former comrades from Papa's party, warned him that his name was already on a black list of those who were to be arrested. That same day, he took my brother and disappeared without saying goodbye. At night the secret police came to our house. The men forced their way into my room, searched it without finding anything, and left.

Again and again, I think what a difficult decision it must have been for Papa to flee with Helmut and to leave my mother and me behind.

I believe the instructions about how she should illegally follow him to France were included in a letter that arrived from Paris a few weeks later. His directives were written between the regular lines with the use of urine as ink. My mother could read them with help from a friend by holding the pages over a candle flame. I am not sure of any of this; perhaps it exists only in my imagination. It's quite possible that his instructions concerning our escape were transmitted via one of those former party members. When my mother received the letter, she started selling our furniture, household goods, and the firewood. With the proceeds from this sale and with help from father's friends, she barely managed to scrape together the money we needed for our trip.

On the day of our departure, December 21, a relative helped us take our suitcases on a cart from Rechenfeldstraße to the Teichmanns' house. This had to be done at night so we wouldn't arouse any suspicion. It was very cold. My mother and I were to take the earliest local train to Vienna's Westbahnhof and transfer to the express train to Germany. Saying goodbye to Aunt Anni was very moving. The remembrance of it still depresses me. She and my mother must have been sure that they would never see one another again.

Whenever I visit Austria, I am drawn back to Purkersdorf. One late morning in autumn, I was walking through the woods toward Rudolfshöhe as I had done when I was a child hunting for mushrooms and gathering firewood. I didn't hold back my tears on this saunter through the rustling leaves.

Chapter 6

THE ESCAPE TO FRANCE

Several relatives on my father's side were expecting us at the Westbahnhof in Vienna. Even though I remember their faces only dimly, I'm sure my aunts Dora and Pepi were among them. Our farewells had to take place very discreetly. As I was stepping into the compartment, I noticed that Aunt Rosi, my father's younger sister, and her daughter, my little cousin Lizzi, accompanied us.

It is impossible for me to bring back to mind what I felt as the train pulled out of the station, but I can imagine my emotions: apprehension, fear, and a great sadness. My aunts who had shown me so much affection stayed behind on the platform. Perhaps they had no idea where we were going. And I? Was I aware of our circumstances? That it would be a journey without return? I'm quite sure I was. The mood at our goodbyes and the fact that we left an empty home behind in Purkersdorf said enough, even to a ten-year-old boy.

On the train, we had to act as though we didn't know each other, and there was to be no conversation either. We had taken just a few pieces of luggage to prevent anybody from suspecting that we might be moving or taking off on a long trip. In case of difficulties, our relatives had to remain incognito, and our intention had to be even more secret. As we were passing by Purkersdorf, Aunt Anni and Uncle Rudolf waved a final farewell. A little later the train was speeding by the Haaghof in Neulengbach. No signs of a farewell there. Did Grandfather know of our escape or of my father's flight with Helmut? Perhaps. Who knows?

Our destination was Karlsruhe in Germany, near the French border. When I took the same route in 1989 to commemorate fifty years of exile, the train made a stop in St. Pölten, speedily passed by

Mauthausen, where the most horrible concentration camp in Austria had been located, as if it were trying to avoid the past, and then stopped again at Linz, Salzburg, and Munich. The schedule in 1938 must have been similar. I remember that the trip was uneventful. We didn't need passports since Austria had been annexed by Germany.

We arrived in Karlsruhe not too late in the afternoon, transferred to a train that went along the border, and reached Wörth, a small town ten miles outside of Karlsruhe on the other side of the Rhine. On my trip fifty years later, I remembered, strangely enough, the art-nouveau style of the station and knew exactly from which track the local would depart.

The station at Wörth consisted of just the small cabin of the gatekeepers who were the contacts for the man who would take us across the border. According to my brother who, at my father's side, had experienced the same thing a few weeks earlier, these men had kept their allegiance to the Social Democratic Party, even though they wore SA uniforms and, for appearance's sake, uttered anti-Semitic insults. They dealt with us the same way, but without the insults, just dry instructions. Aunt Rosi and my mother stepped into the little hut and stayed there a while. Lizzi and I had to wait outside. We were afraid. After nightfall a middle-aged German showed up: our guide. His fee was negotiated behind closed doors. A little later we set off.

It was a very cold night, with snow everywhere. Loaded down with all our possessions, we followed the man silently across open country. He was in a hurry. It was a three-hour trek. As we approached the border, we had to be very cautious. German soldiers were constantly sweeping the area with search lights mounted on watch towers. We cowered in a ditch to wait for the right moment to run ahead one by one. "Now!" said the man in a muffled voice after a cone of light had passed over us.

On the French side, we had to cross a high embankment that was guarded by the local police. We waited for the right moment, and a little later we were walking up a steep road toward the small village of Lauterbourg. We were in France, even if not as yet safely so, as we were soon to realize.

It was close to midnight. Following the instructions my mother had been given, we looked for the house of a Jewish family named Levy. This is where weeks ago Father and Helmut had spent the night. The Levys, we thought, would put us up and help us get to Strasbourg. After we had knocked many times, a woman at last looked out of a window on the second floor. She was almost hysterical when she said she couldn't help us and that we should go away because the authorities were very strict and would punish us and send us back to Germany. Lizzi started to cry and so did I. Yes, I had tried long enough to act like a good little boy and not give Mama any trouble. Before the woman closed her window, she suggested that we look for the local electrician, who had a car and could take us to Strasbourg. And he did indeed help us.

A short time later, the car was speeding down a straight, tree-lined road as fast as it would go. I still remember this drive vividly! When we arrived in the city, the man dropped us off at the rear entrance of a hospital run by a religious order. My mother gave him our last money. After we explained our situation, the nuns took us in. Mama and Aunt Rosi were put up in the women's section. My mother told us later that the next day the nurses had insisted on examining her and taking her temperature. I don't know where they took Lizzi; I was admitted to a small sickroom where I joined three wheezing old men. One of them died during the night. He was covered with a linen cloth before they moved him out. The next day we had to leave very early, no doubt to avoid potential complications. The nuns gave us a breakfast of milk and perhaps my first French croissant.

There was still the dangerous possibility even in Strasbourg that we might be sent back to Germany. My mother and Aunt Rosi went to a Jewish organization that would help us get to Paris. On this day, a benefactor, perhaps a member of this organization or of the Social Democratic Party, invited us to dinner at a restaurant. I no longer am sure what we were served, but the ambiance of that French restaurant has stayed with me very clearly, probably also because I had never eaten in a restaurant before. That same day we took the train to Paris.

As we were entering the city, the engine got stuck in snow, and we along with the other passengers had to walk to a Métro station. This is how we made it to the Gare de l'Est. There Papa, Uncle

Max, and my brother were waiting for us. We were safe.

When I think of this odyssey, I can imagine the great fear my father must have felt, wondering if our escape to France would be successful.

About fifteen years ago, I visited my cousin Lizzi in Val d'Or, a small town in northern Canada. It had been my hope to exchange a few reminiscences with her. But my little Lizzi's memory was badly frayed. She was very hesitant to talk about those days, and so I didn't insist. But she did tell me that she had been interned for deportation at Drancy near Paris when an Austrian officer had the fortunate idea to save her because she was from Vienna. He got Lizzi out of the camp, and she spent the rest of the war hiding out at the homes of friends and relatives. Her parents, my aunt Rosi and uncle Max, were arrested at the Swiss border and deported to the extermination camp at Auschwitz.

In 1989, during that journey into the past, I arrived in Wörth at sundown, exactly as I had fifty years ago. I didn't think I could walk the ten miles to Lauterbourg and rode the bus. I took a good look at the people, most of them older men, each one of whom could have been our guide. The bus stopped in every village. People exchanged greetings, some in German, others in French. The trip took one hour, and I got off on the German side of Lauterbourg. When I raised my hand at the little border post to say hello, they did nothing but look at me with indifference. There was the embankment, but this time without guards. I went into town to see if I could locate the house of the Jewish family. There was nothing I recognized. I was very moved. It was a Monday. I walked through the nearly empty streets, trying to hide my tears. It is strange how quickly feelings I had suppressed come to life again even many years later. I was hungry, but couldn't find a place to eat that was open. At last I saw on the main street of the village behind scaffolding the façade of a house that seemed to be a restaurant. The door was open. The only person there was the owner. She told me they were closed on Mondays. Nonetheless, she served me a delicious fish Alsatian style and I ordered a bottle of wine to go with it. A few weeks later, I found out that the restaurant was the famous *La Poëlle d'Or*, a three-star place that on weekends is frequented by gourmets from all over the world. I tried to make conversation and talk a little about those days, but my throat felt as if I was being strangled. I spent the night at a guesthouse since the only hotel in town had an atmosphere that didn't agree with my emotions.

The next day I went to the station to take the eight-o'clock train to Strasbourg. On my way I passed the Jewish cemetery, the extent of which surprised me. No doubt the community had been very numerous and important, which would also explain why Lauterbourg was one of the places that fleeing Jews chose to cross over into France. In Strasbourg I looked in vain for the hospital of the nuns. I wanted to thank them in some way, which, given my emotional state, would have been difficult, however.

I went for a walk through the center of town, bought a jacket, and ended up in one of the many restaurants, thinking of the dinner we had had with our anonymous benefactor.

Chapter 7

PARIS

In the Rue de l'Aqueduc there is a small hotel by the same name where we spent nine months. Several of its rooms were occupied by emigrants, who, like us, spoke little or no French. Whenever I think of those first days in Paris, a joke that was popular among Jews who were hanging on to what was left of their sense of humor pops into my mind:

> A knock at the door of a shabby hotel.
> Voice inside: "Qui est il?"
> Voice outside: "Je."
> Voice inside: "Te?"
> Voice outside: "Me!"
> Voice inside: "Come on in, Moishe!"

We lived in a rather small room with two double beds. From the window one could see the jumble of train tracks near the Gare du Nord. At the corner across the street was a fire station, with squad cars and fire trucks with sirens pulling out frequently. There was always something interesting to watch.

Near the Hôtel de l'Aqueduc was a school in which my brother and I were enrolled. Despite our different ages, we were put in the same class. For lunch we received a simple *déjeuner*, with a spoonful of marmalade for dessert. During recess we learned "*aux osselets*," a game of skill for which we needed tiny little pig bones we could get for free at the butcher shop. We played "*aux boules*" (marbles) or "temple hopping." Our ignorance of the French language was a serious problem in all subjects but math and geography. The teachers insisted that their students memorize (*par coeur*) a summary of the class. I still remember the résumés in history, which I learned by rote in long torturous hours after having tried to understand what they said. Even though in general we were treated rather courteously, there was one teacher who sometimes made us recite what we had committed to memory in front of the giggling class. Another assignment was to draw maps of France and to add rivers, cities, and other geographical characteristics. I was very good at that. Even today I can reproduce the outlines of France quite precisely. I also learned penmanship, with emphasis on the downward strokes. We had swimming lessons in an indoor pool whose obnoxious chlorine smell was new to me and has never left my nose.

My father had to renew our residence permit, I believe, every week – a ridiculous chicanery enforced by the France of that time. The lines outside the police prefectures extended for several blocks. The number of refugees increased day after day. One of them was Leopold Stern, an advocate of adult education in Vienna, a poet, story teller, and dramatist, who returned to Vienna after the war and died there in 1966. The poem of his that impressed me the most is titled "The Beggars":

> The Beggars
> Have there ever been cathedrals without steps
> And have these steps ever been free of beggars?
> The poor lift up the palms of their hands,
> Their bodies sickly and anguish in their eyes,
> And plead for alms when the organs call.
>
> This time also has its cathedrals
> And its beggars, but on different steps.
> Before offices, anguish in their eyes,
> The exiles line up – Louvre, have them painted! –
> And plead for permits when the clerks summon.
>
> Before each door the boots of soldiers.
> In every file the traces of sighs,
> Yessir; a thumb print and the dates.

And their transgression? They were democracy's
Beggars for freedom before the prefectures.

(From: *Die hundert Hefte*, No. 19, by
Josef Luitpold, New York, 1944)

    My father trained to become an electrician so that he could show a practical skill in case there was a country that would accept us. New Zealand at that time was offering visas to technical specialists. To emigrate there was an option, though not a very realistic one. I don't think Father pursued his training for long.
    We explored Paris on long walks, taking the Métro only on special occasions. I'm not sure where Papa got the money to see us through, but I assume that there were leftist organizations with international support to help comrades who had fled to Paris and that there were similar Jewish institutions. It's not surprising that my father more than once suffered from severe headaches that forced him to stay in bed for several days. And sometimes, in the evening, with great caution he opened his violin case and played his instrument, one of the most beloved things he had succeeded in keeping during his flight.
    The French celebrate Bastille Day with a great deal of enthusiasm. During the night of July 14, surprised by so much euphoria, we experienced the demonstrations of Liberté-Fraternité-Egalité by the Parisians. We tried to share in the general rejoicing. My parents danced to the rhythm of a French waltz and drank wine. Songs like "Douce France," "Pigalle," and "J'attendrais" were popular that year. The warm voice of Edith Piaf was heard over all the loudspeakers.
    Those few light moments were overshadowed by the events in Eastern Europe, portents of a dramatic future: the occupation of Czechoslovakia, the German politics of expansion, and the news about the alarming outrages the Nazis were committing against the Jews. My father, I am sure, was terribly worried about the welfare of his various relatives in Austria. Aunt Rosi, Uncle Max, my cousin Lizzi, and we were safe in Paris, at least for the time being. One can easily imagine how much our own uncertain fate preyed on Papa's mind.

Some of the Red Falcons in Paris, 1939; from l. to r.: Dorli Loebl (deported from France to Auschwitz, Aug./Sept. 1942); Madeleine (Lene) Pariser (survived hidden near Montauban); Steffi Bauer; Gerhard (Koinikoff) Kohn, Herbert Schiller, Hanspeter Semrad, partially covered by Peter Ackermann, with cap (escaped to the United States), Marianne Pollak (suicide in Vienna after the war); Otti Bauer, (brother of Steffi Bauer); Peter Berczeller; Adèle Kurzweil (deported from France to Auschwitz); Hilde Schlesinger (lives in San Francisco)

In August 1939, Uncle Schwarz, Aunt Dora, and my cousin Fredi came to say goodbye. They were on their way to the United States, with a stopover in London to look in on Robert who had been able to flee Austria on a *Kindertransport*. We didn't know if we would see each other again. Fredi reminded me recently that my brother was sick and to everybody's horror suddenly sat up in bed and vomited a stream of blood. Fortunately, it was merely an internal nosebleed. At another time, I sleepwalked, which did not happen again in my whole life, and urinated on my parents' bed. Fear and stress, I realize, express themselves in strange ways.

On the initiative of Marianne Pollak, a Social Democrat from Austria, an association with the name of "Group Friendship" or

The Robinsonians in Plessis-Robinson, 1939; from left to right: Bruno Schwebel, Walter Grün, Gerhard Kohn, Gustl Papanek, Herbert Schiller, Kurt Sonnenfeld (Kugerl), Joseph Polzer

"Red Falcons Group" was formed at the end of 1938. In all probability, my father too had something to do with this organization. The group, which my brother and I joined, was made up of children between the ages of eight and fourteen; only half of them were Jews. Its core consisted of Heinz Leichter, Peter Ackermann, Adèle Kurzweil, Joseph Polzer, Herbert Schiller, Hilde Schlesinger, Ernst (Schneckerl) Weisselberg, Hanspeter Semrad, Kurt (Kugerl) Sonnenfeld, Dorli Löbl, Gerhard Kohn (whom we called Koinikoff), Rosi Foscht, Gustl Papanek, Lene Pariser, Hanna Kaiser (who married Gustl Papanek) as well as Helmut and Bruno Schwebel. I remember only a few of them. As far as I know, almost all of them were able to escape from France. Adèle Kurzweil – more about her fate in chapter 10 – was deported to Auschwitz. Dorli Löbl and Ernst Weisselberg did not survive either. As a group we participated in the interment of the Socialist leader Otto Bauer.

We spent the summer vacation of 1939 in Plessis-Robinson south of Paris in an old villa with a large garden. The activities of the Red Falcons were coordinated by Walter Grün with whom I

Father between Walter Grün (r.) and Karl Wernert at
Camp Meslay du Maine, fall 1939

have maintained – here in Mexico – a cordial and close friendship during the past sixty years. We took part in games of all kinds. The performance of a shadow play comes to mind in which the actors appeared as silhouettes on a taut linen cloth. We put on comedies – I played the joker – and Walter organized readings. But there was also political instruction. We were made aware of the reasons for our exile. We memorized and sang the "Internationale" and other workers' songs and firmly believed in the victory of international socialism. Even today these songs move me and I sing along spontaneously whenever I hear them. After our sojourn in Plessis-Robinson, we were also called the "Robinsonians".

On September 1 of that year, the Germans marched into Poland. Two days later, England and France declared war on Germany – passively, for the time being.

I don't know how and when I learned that Papa together with all Austrian and German men, no matter what their political sympathies, had been ordered to report to the large Vélodrome d'Hiver. From there he was sent to the internment camp of Meslay du Maine in Normandy, where he was registered as a *prestataire étranger* and was granted the right to asylum. At the same time, he was obligated to perform military service for France, something that never happened. In Meslay alone, there were close to 3,000 internees.

One day after the German invasion of Poland, my brother and I along with other Robinsonians were moved to a house for Jewish refugee children north of Paris.

Chapter 8

MONTMORENCY

(I owe the information that enabled me to complete this chapter to the book by Ernst Papanek, *Out of the Fire* (New York: Morrow, 1975). I also relied on the (unpublished) recollections of Käthe Bodek and on conversations with my brother, with Hanna and Gustl Papanek, and with Kurt Sonnenfeld.)

Shortly after September 1, 1939, Helmut and I together with several other Red Falcons were taken from Plessis-Robinson to an O.S.E. refugee home in Montmorency, a northern suburb of Paris. This organization had appointed Ernst Papanek, a leader of Austria's Young Socialists, to supervise their children's homes. The older boys were housed at the historic Chateau Les Tourelles, which had recently been reopened, while the girls were sent to the so-called Villa Helvetia – even though they protested their separation from the boys.

I don't know why my brother and I were at first sent to the Villa Helvetia. Perhaps because this home had been designated to accommodate younger children like myself – I was eleven at the time – and because they didn't want to separate my brother and me. I can imagine, at any rate, how disappointing it must have been for him not to stay with the older Robinsonians at Les Tourelles. While I don't remember if Mother went with us, it is possible that she was allowed to work with Käthe Bodek who had been employed in February to run the kitchen. It would have been traumatic for Mama if she had been forced in such uncertain times to remain in Paris by herself. A little later, though, she was sent to Les Tourelles where she worked as a cook.

The Villa Helvetia was located on the Rue de Valmy in a

Château Les Tourelles

neighborhood of mansions hidden behind walls. The main house with its turrets and skylights – a run-down former hotel – was surrounded by meadows and a small forest full of doves, sparrows, and other kinds of birds. It was being refurbished, thanks to financial support from rich French Jews, especially from the Baronesse de Gunzbourg and members of the Rothschild family, to shelter about one hundred children. The O.S.E. sponsored another nine houses, among them the Villa La Guette where my cousins Herbert, Dita, and Nelly, children of my father's brother Oskar, were placed.

I don't know why I had always believed that Helmut and I spent the nine months in Montmorency at the Villa Helvetia. It came as a great surprise to me to hear from Kugerl Sonnenfeld that things had been different. My memory had made Les Tourelles and Villa Helvetia one and the same.

I am equally uncertain about the length of our stay at the Villa Helvetia before we were transferred to Les Tourelles where we rejoined the other Robinsonians. At that time, my mother was already working in the kitchen.

Following socialist tradition, our activities were arranged in a way that gave the older children a say in all decisions affecting their affairs. Our daily routine started at seven o'clock when we got up, did exercises outdoors, ran a few laps around the property, washed, and had breakfast. After that we did school work and chores and played. The meadows and trees were the right place to go bowhunting for birds – the cord for the bow string was a much-desired bartering object – or we played cops-and-robbers and hide-and-seek. It was an enjoyable activity on many nights to scare the girls with linen capes and lanterns. There were some kids with leadership qualities, like John from the group of "Cubans" and Günther, a young sportsman we all admired, who was later killed in the Holocaust. Kugerl reminded me that we played on a soccer team and had games against the home at Eaubonne: my brother and he as forwards and I as the goalie. I hope I played better than five years later in Mexico on a team at the Polytechnic. My cousin Herbert, though living at the children's home La Guette, sometimes played on our team. Ernst Papanek's wife, Lene, who was in charge of medical affairs, doctored our "battle wounds."

We were always busy. I was taught how to mend clothing, above all how to darn socks and how to knit. I managed to produce half a mitten, a strange-looking thing without a thumb, and I envied those kids who knew how to be excused from such activities. All I'd be able to accomplish these days is one knit row and perhaps one even more crooked purl row. Our food was good and plentiful so that it didn't take long before I gained weight. I have kept an O.S.E. brochure with a photo that shows me as I am about to bite into a sandwich. On some days Ernst Papanek came to wish us "Bon appétit, les enfants." During one lunch, I vomited my dessert of rice pudding with raisins to see if my mother would come and coddle me. She came running out of the kitchen to find out what was the matter with me. Kugerl told me that my mother gave him a tidbit whenever he came to look for her in the kitchen, the same as she did with me, I'm sure. The children's and the staff's birthdays were celebrated with cake and presents, mine too, a couple of weeks after we arrived at Villa Helvetia? Quite possibly.

Once a week we were given a bath and sometimes – I don't know why, being ten years old at that time – one of the service staff insisted on scrubbing me down from head to toe with a sponge. Could I have been that dirty? I remember an emotional mixture of wanting to escape, of modesty, and pleasure. For the first time in my life I was surrounded by other naked boys and therefore tempted to compare butts and dicks. At night in our dormitory we played "full moon." To this day I see a freckled behind – was it Kugerl's? – which illuminated the room from an upper bunk.

We found a few instruments at the chateau and used them to start an orchestra. We sang "Lundi matin . . . ," "Madame la Marquise," and other tunes, among them a number of Jewish songs like "Hava nagila." I remember how much joy it gave me to participate in the canon "Frère Jacques" and that I hid when the folk dancing started. I'm sure my brother had similar experiences, but we never got around to talking about them. Käthe Bodek mentions in her memoirs that I was a great success playing a circus clown in a magnificent theatrical performance that a certain Boris Ginodmann directed. "I can't help laughing when I think back to the time chubby Bruno Schwebel was dressed up as a clown," Käthe writes. My first attempts as a comedian?

For a short time I and some other children were sent to a nearby public school, where we entered classes that had already started and where we had to learn a different way of doing division than we were used to in Austria. Also, a classmate taught me that babies were produced when Papa peed into the place where Mama's pee comes from. How long did I believe this kind of wisdom? I'm not sure.

The children in Montmorency were basically divided into three groups: the orthodox Jews, the Robinsonians, and the "Cubans." It is logical that the orthodox were distinguished by their adherence to religious traditions. They prayed on all possible occasions, their food was kosher, they wore yarmulkes, and they hardly ever mingled with the others. For me, they were children from a different world. I never tired of watching them.

About half the Robinsonians were of non-Jewish background. What made us different from the other kids was our political attitude. The victory of socialism had been instilled in us and also that we were part of an international movement which fought the Nazis. I, however, showed little interest in politics. I was much too busy being a good boy and gaining the affection of the others. My preference was for warmth and tenderness.

The "Cubans" were children from that group of a thousand unfortunates who had succeeded in May 1939 in escaping from

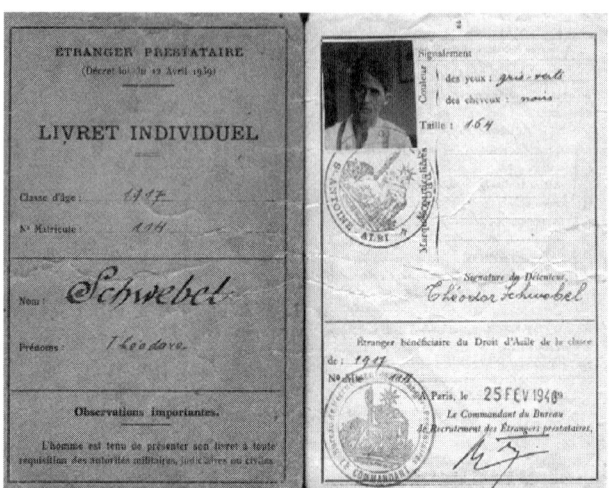
Father's identification as "Étranger Prestataire"

German concentration camps and who, sailing to Cuba aboard the *St. Louis*, had hoped to be given asylum there. Even though their papers were in order, the Cuban authorities denied them permission to disembark, citing legal irregularities. After they had tried without success to find refuge in the United States, the majority of them registered on the quota list of U.S. Immigration, these "Wandering Jews" had to return to Europe. Understandably, they could no longer go back to their native countries of Austria or Germany. They were put ashore in Rotterdam; 227 of them were taken to France. The adults were sent to a French camp near Le Mans, the children were admitted into the O.S.E. homes: the girls to Eaubonne, a new home at La Chênaie, the boys first to the Villa Helvetia and later to Les Tourelles, where we were. Few of them survived the Shoah.

For all our different backgrounds, we had a good rapport with most of the children. What united us was the fear of an uncertain future, also the fact that we were separated from our parents, knowing nothing about them. But there were occasional discussions between the older Robinsonians and the Cubans, this group usually rather short on political convictions.

During those days we briefly saw our father after he had been

Este muchacho de la OSE saborea su bocadillo aún antes de haberle hincado el diente

[Bruno Schwebel, from an O.S.E brochure, 1939]

given permission at the internment camp of Meslay to visit his family. I remember a very emotional reunion that was overshadowed, however, by the tense political circumstances. At the end of April, he was ordered to return and he reported back at his camp on May 8, 1940.

Two days later, the German invasion of Holland and Belgium began; the rhetorical war was over – the phony war, as the English called it, "drôle de guerre" for the French – the real war had started. We no longer went to school. Together with the adults, we followed the German advance on a large map.

Aerial attacks by the *Luftwaffe* were expected any moment. At the home we practiced evacuation drills. Sirens were wailing almost every day, whereupon we had to run to the basement *("Alerte!")*. We had to be down there in two minutes or less, for which reason we kept our clothes and shoes ready by our bedside. During one of these exercises, I stayed back in bed with a kitten we had adopted until Mama came and got me, bawling me out as she took me to the basement. That whole part of the building had been converted into an air-raid shelter with a store of food, water, flashlights, medicine, and other things needed in an emergency. This was a place where we sang the songs we had learned and also broke into the Marseillaise. All the children helped to black out the Villa's windows. In the garden, we dug trenches and fortified them with sand bags in case we had to abandon the building and seek shelter elsewhere.

Everybody was deeply afraid the Germans might use poison gas. We were supplied with rudimentary masks which had a distinctive smell of rubber and insecticide, and we were instructed to run against the wind in case of an attack. Years later in Mexico, I experienced severe chest tightness upon entering a movie theater until I realized that the hall had been disinfected with a chemical that smelled like those gas masks.

Rumors that the Nazis were coming to kill us increased the feeling of frightful anxiety. All over France the "news" was circulating that the German airplanes would be dropping poisoned candy and exploding fountain pens. We were strictly forbidden to pick up any discarded objects, including the grenade fragments some of the kids had found in the garden. But we were lucky. Even though the sirens whined every night to warn of an air attack, no bombs were dropped in our vicinity. There was also no major damage from the bombardments in Paris, although there were reports of over 1,500 fatalities.

Belgium surrendered on May 28, and a week later we heard the roar of guns from the battle approaching Paris. At night we saw the detonations of bombs and mortar shells that lit up the horizon, and we could feel the ground shake under our feet. We saw more than one plane being shot down.

Montmorency was the last stronghold of the French. Paris fell on June 14, 1940, which ended the military activities. The chains of German tanks had ground down French pride and those principles of liberté–égalité–fraternité which had been proclaimed 150 years before.

I have returned to Montmorency several times. Les Tourelles I bypassed, my memory of it having become blurred. I had some difficulty finding the Villa Helvetia. The place had been completely renovated and transformed into business offices. I was too agitated to ask for permission to enter and instead merely looked through an opening in the gate. The same birds were pecking on the lawn, there were the same turrets, the windows to the dormitories, now new and shiny, the same annex where the girl Robinsonians had slept. In place of the little forest, there was now a police station. No one knew that fifty years ago this building had granted refuge to Jewish children, many of whom did not survive.

Chapter 9

FLIGHT FROM PARIS

We were still at Les Tourelles when the German army had advanced to less than twenty miles north of Paris. Just in time before our evacuation, all children had been given a tote bag to carry their few belongings, also a gas mask and a ration of dark chocolate.

Ernst Papanek had negotiated with the French authorities for a train that would evacuate the children of the O.S.E. homes to southern France. The majority of them were to be taken to Montintin, a chateau to be rented with money donated by the O.S.E. sponsors. Montintin was located in central France near Limoges, a city with a left-leaning administration that was willing to help Ernst Papanek in his efforts to move the children to a safe place.

But Paris was total chaos. The authorities were unable to keep their promise. On June 6, after intensive discussions between the directors of O.S.E. and the Ministry of Social Services, it was agreed to add one freight car to the train departing for Limoges. One single car for hundreds of children? Thanks to the tenacious labors of O.S.E., the undersecretary, a socialist by the name of Chabaud, finally offered to put together a special train that was to leave the next day from the Gare d'Austerlitz. In the end, the promised special train consisted of not more than two freight cars. So much for this promise.

I don't know who managed to get out on this transport. Witnesses report that it was completely overcrowded, with people clinging to anything they could get their hands on. It must have been June 8 or 9, very early in the morning, when all the children from the homes were loaded into the available vehicles. My brother and I and some other Robinsonians were penned up in a black delivery van with only a few small windows. Lack of space forced us to leave most of our possessions behind. What was left of the chocolate was distributed among us. I filled my pockets with my share. Mother stayed behind crying.

When I think back to that farewell scene, I find it difficult to suppress the tears I probably didn't shed back then. We had no idea when we might be reunited or even where my father was. An uncertain future was ahead of us. We were among the last of the children to leave Montmorency.

I found a place near one of the windows, which helped me to control my nausea. As we drove through Paris, there was smoke everywhere. Only later did we learn that the French had created an artificial layer of smoke to keep German plane crews from recognizing certain landmarks. The main road to Orléans, barely sixty miles south of Paris, was clogged with thousands of people in cars, trucks, busses, carts, and bicycles or on foot. We joined the crowd and made only very slow headway.

Late in the morning, German dive bombers, their engines roaring, attacked the column of civilians with machine guns. Our truck stopped; we sought protection under a church portal. Several vehicles went up in flames; people were left lying in the street. None of us was injured, however.

At nightfall, when we could see Orléans ahead, the fighter bombers returned. We ran into a grain field in order to hide, and we witnessed the air attack on the city. We waited in our hideout until the next morning, hoping to pass through Orléans and get out of harm's way. Clouds of smoke were rising from the direction of the railroad station and the *centre de ville*. They told us later that these were the most heavily damaged areas. We arrived at Limoges, roughly another 130 miles to the south, without further difficulties.

When we got there, the driver had to ask directions to Montintin. Soon we drove along a country road winding its way through woods and meadows toward a hill. We reached our destination around noon, tired and hungry.

Montintin was a medieval chateau, gloomy and gone to ruin, which did not bother us in the least, of course. After what we had been through, exploring the place was a welcome diversion. The building had three stories, a large number of rooms, a knights' hall, and two round towers supported by external pillars. According to Ernst Papanek, the owner, an arrogant count who looked like a caricature of his ilk and a fanatical anti-Semite, wouldn't stand for the presence of Jewish children on his property. But when all was said and done, the directors of O.S.E. succeeded in moving him to lease his chateau for an astronomical sum of cash. When we arrived, the children who had come with Ernst a few days before had already done a tolerable job of cleaning up. We all helped to make the place habitable. That evening we were informed about our situation. Afterward, there was a little time left for playing.

My mother arrived two days later. Since she couldn't take the train, she and some of the Villa Helvetia women (Käthe Bodek, Klari Willner, a certain Rachel, and a few others) had decided to make their way south on foot. I don't know how they obtained the *sauf-conduit* the French authorities required of all adults trying to leave Paris. This form of useless bureaucracy and demeaning treatment of all refugees is something I can't comprehend to this day. Mama clung to whatever vehicle was available and resumed her escape that way. She was even able to take the train from Orléans for the rest of the trip. As is true with my father, I regret today that I didn't talk with her at greater length about the events of that time. But it is also understandable that we, my parents as well as I, refused to revive all these memories.

We stayed at Château de Montintin only four or five days. I don't recall exactly how we managed to cover the fifty miles to Brive-la-Gaillarde, from where a train took us to Montauban, another seventy-five miles farther south. Paris had surrendered by then; a few days later France capitulated and a new government was installed at Vichy.

Forty-two years later, when I repeated the trip from Limoges to Château Montintin, I tried to get into a conversation with the driver of the taxi I had hired at the station. At first I had planned to rent a bicycle, but a look at the map convinced me that I'd not be up to the ride. During the time it took us to get there, the driver kept watching me in his rearview mirror, and I'm sure he had no idea why I had teary eyes and why I wanted to go to this deserted chateau of all places since the children who had spent their

Château de Montintin in 1982

vacations there had left a month ago, Montintin still serving as a hostel for poor Jewish children. On my way I thought of all that had happened after our departure, things I didn't know about until many years later when I was safe in Mexico.

August 26 and 27 were disastrous days in the history of the Jews who happened to be in France at that time, including those who believed they were safe in the Free Zone, like the children from Montintin and other homes. These days were the beginning of the end for many of them, the time when the massive roundups started. With the help of the local police, the Germans swooped down on Montintin, deported the sixty-nine children who had stayed there, and shipped them to the extermination camps. I had probably spent those days at the chateau with some of them. Perhaps we had shared my chocolate, a game, or some laughs. Unfortunately, their faces, their voices, their names have slipped from my memory. One boy only, a youngster named Emil Geisler, was able to survive. I would not be surprised if the chateau's owner was partially responsible for this raid, one of the first in that area.

Klaus Barbie, indicted and sentenced in Lyon forty years later, was the head of the organization which tracked down Jews in the southeast of France and sent them to the death camps. My uncle Max and my aunt Rosi, my beloved aunt, who had fled with us from Austria, suffered that fate.

At the time of the Barbie trial, I was attending a television conference in Geneva and decided on the spur of the moment to travel to Lyon to witness the trial. When I showed my Mexican press credentials at the relevant office, I was unable to express my purpose understandably. I was very nervous, close to tears, and felt I couldn't breathe. Perhaps I appeared too excited or even dangerous to the officials, who wouldn't allow me to enter. I took the train back to Geneva that same day. A feeling of frustration and failure has been with me ever since.

One must never forget the heroes of the French Resistance, the *maquisards*, especially Maurice Richard who was shot at Mauthausen. They were able to save many lives! The leaders of the resistance within O.S.E. were Dr. Eugène Minkovski and Jenny Masour, who directed their rescue operations from Paris.

The taxi drove slowly through the rain and let me enjoy the countryside, gentle hills, richly green. Had we noticed the beauty of this area in those days? When we arrived, the driver stayed in his car, smoking. Our agreement was that he would wait for me half an hour. It stopped raining. Everything was quiet. I started recognizing a few places: the tower where an entertaining afternoon had been arranged for us, the large hall that I looked into through a grimy window. I tried to enter, but all entrances had been locked. Complete silence, moss-covered walls, muddy paths, leaky roof, signs in Hebrew I couldn't read. I experienced the chateau as a huge tombstone for all who had been murdered. Again and again, I saw before me the scene of the children being dragged toward the trucks.

Back at the Limoges station – it was crowded with young hikers and their backpacks. In a certain way I envied them. Perhaps some of them had planned to make camp near Montintin. Perhaps someone would tell them what had happened there. So I hoped in defiance of what I know.

Chapter 10

MONTAUBAN, THE BEGINNING

France was partitioned after its surrender. The North and its operational center of Paris stayed under German control, the South was administered by the so-called Government of France Libre under Marshal Pétain at Vichy. The term "free" for this part of France must be an example of cynicism since its politics, especially concerning the destruction of the Jews and other opponents of the Third Reich, was controlled by the Germans.

Montauban at that time was a small city of about 20,000 inhabitants. But it is also known that for the duration of the greatest crisis more than 150,000 people lived there, seeking protection from fascism. The large majority of them were Spanish Republicans who had fled to the south of France after they had lost the Civil War in April 1939. Knowing that the city would be unable to house that many people, the mayor, a Social Democrat by the name of Fernand Bales, had straw distributed in the streets.

When we arrived at the Gare de Montauban, we encountered the greatest disarray – bundles and pieces of luggage everywhere, filth, and people, lots of people, people who were waiting in line for something or who were camped in the halls of the station. The hissing conversations of the Spaniards were my first encounter with their language. We were expected by someone from the aid committees, which were staffed mostly by our political supporters. I remember that Bruno Kurzweil, who arrived in Montauban a few days later with his family, was a great help in taking care of the administrative formalities the French required. (I'll tell about his tragic fate later on.) We were put up in a house near the River Tarn, 19 Rue de la Caunat, I believe. The owner, living there alone, let us have a room, provided we took care of her garden.

This is the reason that my brother and I devoted ourselves to tending vegetables and exploring the city during our first weeks in Montauban. In our spare time, we roamed through the medieval center of town, the Place Nationale with its double arcades and *le marché*, all buildings constructed of brick. The market was teeming with people who tried to buy groceries cheaply or to steal them. How intensely I remember the peaches whose juice squirted out at the slightest touch! The river with its *pont vieux*, its islets, and bays held a special attraction for us. We improvised fishing hooks and joined the others who were trying to supplement their meager meals with fish. In other words, there wasn't much left to catch.

One day we received news that a group of *prestataires* was arriving in Montauban from the north – my father might be among them. I had no recollection of this incident until my brother mentioned it, possibly because I had repressed the image of my father marching under military guard. The column passed by the station. We followed it a couple of miles and called out to Papa from afar. Afterward, we learned that the men were to be interned at the concentration camp of St. Antoine, near Albi, about twenty miles outside of Montauban. Fortunately, the administration of this camp was not handled as inhumanely as that of Septfonds or of the camp whose name resembles a belch: Gurs.

A few days later, we went to St. Antoine and could kiss Papa – through barbed wire. He was emaciated and dirty, his eyes lay deeper in their sockets than ever before. After about a month, on July 24, 1940, he was released and came to be with us in Montauban.

Considering the general lack of accommodations, it was a miracle that Papa and a small group of his friends managed to get us settled in an abandoned farmstead in the hills surrounding the town. Certainly our good relationship with the helpful mayor, Fernand Bales, played a significant role in this. To this day, the area is called Beausoleil, a very appropriate name for a countryside of meadows, vegetable fields, and vineyards with constant sunshine.

Rooms and work on the *ferme* were distributed democratically. My mother would cook for all of us; the others in the group were to procure things to eat. Oskar Braun and his friend Gisela Wintergerst, both of them refugees from the International Brigades in the Spanish Civil War, shared one room, Walter Grün and Klari Willner, activists on the left in Austria, another. There were also three unmarried men: Paul Schick, forty years old and very concerned that his shoes should always look immaculately polished – in 2002 I happened to pass by his grave in the Israelite Cemetery of Vienna – and another man – I think his name was Herbst – bunked in a storage shed. The third, whose name I don't remember and who always carried a book under his arm, slept I don't know where. And we Schwebels settled down in the living room.

We took turns lighting the fireplace in the morning for our first cup of coffee. When it was Herbst's turn, we pretended to still be asleep in order to enjoy the spectacle. He was an intellectual with thick eyeglasses who hadn't the slightest idea how to start a fire. He'd always try to get a flame going by throwing the paper on top of the kindling.

The living room, black from smoke and permanently smelling of bacon, was three things in one: kitchen, dining room and, in the evening, meeting place. All members of the group were leftists of quite different persuasions. Whenever the exchange of political opinions increased in intensity, I preferred to disappear. My father voiced his convictions passionately, and I avoided seeing him in a discussion as much as possible. But sometimes he just got out his violin, which had made it through all internment camps, Mama started to sing, and soon everybody joined in.

Of the friends who did not live on the *ferme,* I have an especially fond memory of Willi Speiser and his wife, Trude, and of Rudi Lepkovitz and his Erna. Rudi and Willi are dead now. I visited Erna in September 2000 and took that occasion to exchange our impressions of those days. She told me about the horrible conditions in the concentration camp of Septfonds, where she was interned in the women's section. Somehow, she had persuaded the commandant to let her go since she was not Jewish. Her husband had been a soccer player in Austria and had the reputation of being quarrelsome. *Bravero,* as we say in Mexico. There are stories about him frequently going to Vienna after the war and causing trouble, especially in beer joints. And when he was in danger of being arrested, he would call himself a Frenchman – and other than that they could "kiss his ass." While the Gestapo was present, openly since the beginning of 1942, Rudi lived for months hidden in a closet and came out only at night. The Speisers and the Lepkovitzes were among the few who managed to survive the Nazi persecutions in Montauban, a town that had granted them refuge and where they stayed to live.

Also Uncle Oskar, Aunt Anni, and my cousins, Dita, Herbert, Nelly, and Alfons, were in Montauban. Peter, the youngest of them, was born there, my aunt having become pregnant at the most inopportune time.

At the *ferme* there was a fig tree which bore large fruit with a light skin, *higos güeros*, as they are called in Mexico, a few apple trees, and a pond with ducks and frogs where I spent many an hour observing the tadpoles, water fleas and other little critters. There was also a latrine which I frequently used on account of the many and easily accessible grapes. The well with a manual pump was the meeting place for our daily ablutions. When it was the women's turn, the volunteer pumper had to avert and close his eyes. This farmstead no longer exists. When I tried to go there in 1997, all I found was a wide construction ditch which is now a superhighway. How much I'd have liked to bite into one of those large figs again and to steal grapes from the vineyard.

Meals were meager. All basic foodstuffs like bread, milk, and meat were rationed. Food coupons were distributed at City Hall, the same amount for locals and for refugees. But often we witnessed quarrels. We had a bicycle, which made shopping in town easier. Once I was sent for bread. When I tried to hand the appropriate coupons to the *boulangère*, she smiled at me tenderly and turned away to serve other customers. Today, more than sixty years later, the bakery is at the same location, with modern equipment, run by the woman's granddaughter. During one of my sojourns in Montauban, I entered her shop with the intention of expressing my gratitude for the kindness her grandmother had shown me, but my throat felt parched. I could not say a word. Close to tears, I pointed at a small cake, one from a large selection. As I left, I chewed on my cake and on my frustration.

On another shopping trip into town, I lost a hundred-franc bill. Using flashlights, we looked and looked everywhere I had walked. Feelings of guilt weighed on my conscience for years to come. I was well aware what this money had meant to us.

Often we roamed across the fields, stole grapes (especially the delicate ones that were being protected against frost), nuts and various kinds of fruit, or we went to a creek, Le Tescou, to gather sweetwater mussels. My mother wasn't exactly overjoyed with our harvest because as a good Austrian she had no idea about how to prepare these disgusting little things. Sometimes we even pulled in a little fish that was trying to snatch a fly from the hook we were dangling over the water. Almost every day, I was sent for skim milk to a neighboring farm where it took considerable skill to get past the geese that were guarding the entrance. In times of severe shortages, we cut stinging nettles, which grew everywhere, and boiled them. They tasted like spinach. Another popular food was Jerusalem artichoke, a tuber that was planted in great abundance as food for pigs. When eaten with vinaigrette, it didn't taste bad at all.

At the time of the grape harvest, the vintners had no trouble finding cheap day laborers. Competition for jobs in the Beausoleil area was tough because of the many, primarily Spanish unemployed. I was always turned away, but my fourteen-year-old brother was hired often enough. In the vineyards of Beausoleil, he found his first love, Pilar. I'll never forget the kind of camaraderie prevalent among the Spanish refugees from fascism. They always exchanged friendly greetings and were willing to share their few belongings.

During vacation I watched the sheep and a few cows for an old peasant named Massip. My pay was one quart of milk and the food I ate: bacon, potatoes and cabbage. His wife would usually fill my plate saying: *"Allez manger, mon petit."* I remember the bellwether who obviously considered me a rival and who, with his head lowered, bumped into me at the most unexpected moments. One day somebody gave me a little flute from which I tried to coax a melody while watching the animals. But when a snake turned up, darting its tongue in and out with its head raised, I quickly called it quits.

The Ancien Collège was located where the path leading to the *ferme* met the road to Albi, twenty minutes from our place. As in Paris earlier, my brother and I were put into the same grade. There I finished my last year of elementary school. We had an unforgettable teacher, Monsieur Bigère, who followed the call of his profession with great devotion and used every opportunity to lament France's sad and humiliating decline. He was a patriot and had us line up in the schoolyard and sing the Marseillaise at the beginning and at the end of classes. When my brother visited him thirty years later, M. Bigère emerged from the door of his house, of course wearing his béret, and shouted without hesitation: "Helmut! . . . Et Bruno, où est-il?"

After school we threw stones at the broken windows of an old factory, went fishing where the Canal du Midi empties into the Tarn, kicked a soccer ball around, played boccia – what happiness to own a *sac de boules*! – or explored the banks of the Tescou, where we had to stay away from an old woman prowling the neighborhood, a crazy nymphomaniac, according to those who know such things. Suitable enlightenment about this inclination, in tandem with a song about a lustful girl from Valencia – "Valencienne, fleur de lys, écarte tes cuissses pour que j'enfonce ma saucisse" ("Girl from Valencia, my lily, open your thighs so that I can push my sausage in") – contributed significantly toward my education in matters sexual.

Afternoons my brother and I went to an art school in the center of town. We made drawings of Greek heads or of French historical personalities from sculptures the students themselves had created. I was especially proud of Voltaire's head, the drawing of which I have saved among my odds and ends to this day.

After half a year on the *ferme*, my father found work with a farmer, Monsieur Olier, whose farm extended along the old road to Albi near the Tescou, less than half a mile outside the edge of town. The man let us have one room and gave us permission to raise chickens. I remember that my father wrung the neck of more than one of them. We did miss living with our friends on the *ferme*. But we had a black-and-white fox terrier we called Toutou. He had shown up one day, full of scabies and worms, which Mama took care of, and he was accepted into the family. Papa spent the whole day working at any kind of job in the fields. In the evening, we all went down to the creek to wash. It was the most pleasant time of the day. Sometimes Mother even warbled to herself.

Today Montauban as a tourist destination is insignificant and more than overshadowed by Toulouse and Albi. All the same, I'm drawn back there again and again. I look in on Monsieur Bigère, the art school, the bakery to buy a cake, and imagine returning to the pond on the *ferme*, fishing at the Tarn, or gathering mussels. Every time I visit, I go to the market on the Place Nationale and am disappointed when the juice of the peaches doesn't squirt out after I barely touch them.

Chapter 11

PREPARATIONS IN MONTAUBAN

In the fall of 1941, my father and Walter Grün started to work for an elderly bachelor by the name of Fauche and his two sisters. The Fauches lived outside of Montauban in an old villa, the center of an extensive estate known as Cabarien, which was reached by a narrow road (*la route à Fau*) that crossed the Tescou. In 2000, when I went back there with my wife, Joan, we found a sign attached to the ornate iron gate: "Défense de Passer. Proprieté Privée." We took a look around anyway, even though Mademoiselle de Fauche, of the three siblings the one to live the longest, had died a few years ago.

There stood the old manor house with its flair of bygone grandeur, with the blackened chimneys, the paint on the shutters peeling, ivy, vine creepers, blackberry brambles, and other climbing plants covering the cracks in the old walls. No doubt the Fauches had artistic sensibilities, judging by the statues of fauns, nymphs, and other mythological figures in their gardens. They cultivated flowers, especially roses, and I remember that as a child, when I caught a glimpse of the interior, I could recognize beautiful pictures and paintings. Behind the house were the stables and a garden with a large variety of vegetables, with cherry and orange trees, among others, and further back were the family's large vineyards.

My father had obtained a *carte d'identité* from the Ministry of Labor, which allowed him to be employed by Monsieur Fauche as a farm worker. When I read their contract today, I can only be amazed at the pedantic handwriting of the old gentleman that reveals a good deal about his character. The document, notarized by the signature of Montauban's mayor and by a copious attachment of stamps, describes in such fidelity to detail as to border on the ridiculous what type of work my father and Walter Grün were to perform on and outside the estate. It enumerates down to the minutest particulars the maintenance and care of the fruit trees, the vegetable garden *soignement travaillé* (work to be done diligently), the patio, the horse stables, pigsties, rabbit hutches and chicken coops, the vehicles, water pump, the park, the trails, and the flowers. It is further specified in the contract that fruit has to be harvested, leaves have to be raked, windfall branches gathered, weeds pulled, animals fed, fires lit in stoves and fire places, the entrance as well as the kitchen and hallways of the villa kept clean, and much more. It is pointed out with special emphasis that the employees were to carry out any task they might be asked to perform – a kind of serfdom of the refugees, in other words. Furthermore, they were forbidden to hunt, fish, and pick fruit on the property. And one of them had to be available at all hours of the day. Still, I believe that Monsieur was not quite so exploitive as his contract seems to indicate because we had permission to take from his garden whatever vegetables we needed. Other than that, the man did only what the majority of the farmers in that region also did: he made maximum use of the large supply of refugee labor. Monthly pay was three hundred francs and a 225 liter cask of wine, for both my father and Walter Grün. Ten liters of wine per day for each family! Monsieur Fauche must have assumed that the consumption of wine in Austria is comparable to that in France.

Moving into this environment filled us, including our little dog Toutou, whom we had been allowed to keep, with great expectations. We were assigned a small house behind the villa and a small vegetable garden. Walter Grün and his partner Klari moved into one, we into the other room. There was a latrine, and water had to be hauled in large buckets from a well. We were given permission to keep chickens, rabbits, and a pig, but only one, provided the animals were always properly locked up. I remember that we owned hens, perhaps also rabbits, but I'm sure we didn't have a pig.

The park resembled a small forest and invited exploration. While my father and Walter did their work and Mother took care of the household, my brother and I went to school or took Toutou with us on our excursions. Our Toutou did the most surprising things. He was so agile that he could change directions in midair or come to a complete stop when we called his name. Another of his heroic accomplishments was to steal eggs for us and put them down, one after the other, in front of our feet without breaking them.

Something unique happened at that time: I saw Papa drunk. It happened while he was on his way back from a meeting with friends in town. I remember that he was staggering up the trail to Cabarien at night, his violin under his arm, leaning on Walter – after one of the few and yet so welcome distractions during those tension-filled days.

The Vichy government had accepted the obligation to hand all enemies of the Third Reich over to the Germans – primarily Jews and leftists. This demand became more and more apparent, even from one day to the next, through the presence of the Gestapo and their helpers, the militia and the French police. Ever since my father had joined us in the summer of 1940, he had tried to find a means of escape. It became a priority to obtain visas, no matter for which country. The fact that Father had been an active Socialist gave us hope that an organization like the Second International, The Jewish Labor Committee, The Emergency Rescue Committee, or the Centre Américain de Secours in Marseille might help us. I don't know if he was successful. But it is a fact that individual Americans like Dorothy Borg, Frederick V. Field, and Dr. Muriel Buttinger, who saved countless victims of Nazi persecution, responded to Father's requests. They addressed a series of letters to the American Consulate in Marseille, stating that my father was a farmer and electrician of excellent character and would be a desirable citizen and that his activities had been of a democratic nature and had never been connected with any political movement that was undesirable in the United States. They also pointed out that my mother was an excellent cook and housewife whose greatest desire it was to work in the U.S. These potential benefactors emphasized further that they would be willing to assume full responsibility for us and that we would not cause any problems. In short, we would be ideal immigrants. In May of that year, the Consulate granted us a visa on the condition that we could present tickets for the passage to the U.S. as well as an exit visa for

France. I am sure that my father did not have enough time to meet these conditions, which resulted in an annulment of the North American offer. It is known at the same time that the immigration quota for Europeans was filled by the middle of 1941. The same was true for all other Western countries, which exhausted the opportunities to leave France. In the fall, the chances of escaping deportation were slight. There was only one route to safety left: emigration to Mexico.

The Mexican Consul General in Marseille was Gilberto Bosques (he died in July 1995 at the age of 103), a man of the left and very much attuned to the policies of then president Lázaro Cárdenas. It is a matter of record that the Mexican Embassy in Paris, under the supervision of Luis I. Rodríguez and with support from Gilberto Bosques, between July and December 1940 granted a very large number of visas, both for Spanish Republicans and for many refugees of Central European origin, primarily Germans and Austrians, no matter what their religion.

It was inevitable that my father had to go to Marseille frequently and stay there for a certain time, since the countless required documents had to be obtained in strict sequence:

> Travel document *sauf-conduit* (substitute passport; issued to my father in Montauban on November 6).

> Exit visa from France (likewise issued to my father in Montauban on November 6).

It was our good fortune that the mayor, a Social Democrat by the name of Joseph Bourdeau, who had taken over in February 1941, like his predecessor fully supported issuing documents needed by the refugees in Montauban.

> Entry visa for Mexico, issued by the Mexican Consulate in Marseille on November 6; valid for one year.

> Ship tickets to Mexico via Portugal, paid for by international Jewish organizations. In our case it was Hicem, an organization founded in 1927 that helped

approximately 90,000 Jews to escape via Lisbon.

Entry visa for Portugal, to be paid for on short notice, issued on December 3; valid for thirty days.

Transit visa for Spain, granted on condition that bearer will pass through without delay; issued on December 5.

Exit visa from France via Spain, isssued in Marseille on December 8; valid for one month.

It is obvious that finishing this paper war was my father's highest priority. He had to get this done (*se débrouiller*, as it was called) whichever way he could. In less than a month the transit visa for Spain expired. We went to Marseille more than once. I see myself standing in long lines. Sometimes he had to hide from the police, who were rounding up undocumented people and perhaps also looking for Jews. I'm not sure. That time, the autumn of 1941, left the largest blank space in my memory, I'm sure on account of the tension and anxiety my parents were going through.

As to the aforementioned formalities, any number of stories revolving around them have been told, all of them unbelievably dramatic. As one example, I'd like to mention the case of my uncle Oskar's family. After the Mexican Consulate in Marseille had denied him a visa because he had too many children, five of them, my fourteen-year-old cousin Dita forced her way into Gilberto Bosques's office and weeping went down on her knees, imploring him to reconsider their application. This desperate act saved the lives of her family.

One of the many families who, for reasons unknown to me, could not obtain the visa for Mexico were the Kurzweils: Bruno, who was a great help to us during our sojourn in Montauban; his wife, Gisela; and a girl of seventeen, Adèle, who had been a member of the Robinsonians in Paris and the Villa Helvetia. After that time, Adèle attended the Lycée Michelet in Montauban. In August 1942, the entire Kurzweil family was arrested in Auvillar, a nearby village, sent to the concentration camp of Septfonds, then to Drancy near Paris, and from there they were deported to Auschwitz. One of the tragic facts is that Adèle could have saved herself. She had been offered an opportunity to escape, but she did not want to leave her parents behind in France and went to see them in Auvillar during her fall vacation. In 1994 (yes, 1994!), a suitcase of the Kurzweils with personal items, among them notebooks from that time, were discovered in an abandoned basement used by the Auvillar police department. The French historian Pascal Caïla and Hanna Papanek, Ernst Papanek's daughter-in-law, brought this unbelievable case to public attention. A commemorative plaque in honor of Adèle has now been put up in one of the schoolyards of the Lycée Michelet.

The present-day administration of Montauban, a city with a leftist tradition, sees to it that the current generation is informed about the events of the past. There is a small museum, Musée de la Résistance et de la Déportation, and a Maison du Combattant. There is a tree standing in one of the city squares where the Germans hanged hostages. A memorial tablet attached to it reads: "Français, n'oubliez jamais la barbarie allemande!"

In order to obtain a new visa from the French government after the last one had expired, it was absolutely necessary to have a medical certificate confirming that one did not suffer from a contagious disease. I imagine the French wanted to show the world that their asylum seekers were leaving the country with a clean bill of health. The authorities didn't consider this certificate necessary for those deported to the German extermination camps.

A few days before we left Montauban, around December 25, 1941, Toutou brought us one of the chickens that belonged to Monsieur Fauche, who insisted on having the dog killed. He gave Walter a pistol, who refused to use it, however. The maître himself fired the shot in back of the house, a shot that affected me more than all the bomb explosions I had experienced.

After we had said goodbye to Uncle Oskar and his family – they left France ten weeks later via Marseille – and to our best friends, we left for Pau at the foot of the Pyrenees. Our plan of escape was to leave France for Spain at the border station of Canfranc.

A few weeks later, the villa of the Fauches was occupied by

different residents, by German officers.

During one of my visits to Montauban – it was in 1981 – I and Willi Speiser went to see Mademoiselle de Fauche. I found the ninety-three-year-old lady to be very lively and alert. In contrast to me, she had an incredibly sharp memory. After this very emotional visit, I wrote the story "Mademoiselle de Fauche."

Chapter 12

Story

MADEMOISELLE DE FAUCHE

Wrinkles under a cover of face powder, wilted hands incessantly fidgeting with the folds of a shawl, eyes full of age-old liveliness – that's what has survived of you. The net which holds your rust-red hair together, is it perhaps also a memory aid? A confused edifice of recollections has taken the place of your bones, your flesh, keeps the fragile pieces that remain of your life erect.

In some way I envy you. Everything about you, Mademoiselle de Fauche, is the past. And I, fully in the present, now want to be like you. My memory, you see, has gaps.

I've come back to Montauban. The town hasn't changed much. The bicycles are more beautiful; the Tarn is more polluted. There is a new bridge, and a superhighway has been built over the Route Saint Martial. So many years later, the jukeboxes are still playing "Douce France, souvenir de mon enfance." Even the young people hum its melody. Back then, I believe, there were fewer pretty girls (sure, I was only thirteen) and no boy with a mop of tousled hair and sneakers, of the kind I saw hanging out on the central square. I don't know . . . the dirt was of a different type. Now everything has more polish, more color. Tell me, Mademoiselle, when I look at your France these days with tears in my eyes, and when I see your sky, your garden, is it the gaze of a man who owes a debt?

The same blackberry tendrils along the walls of the Villa de Fauche, growing even wilder. Slowly my body remembers the scratches that were the price for the highest, the blackest berries. It was October then . . . October also now . . . Late roses . . . Perfect quiet! . . . Such a deep blue! . . . And how intense the park's green!

Nothing was green, nothing blue in 1941, times in black-and-white; gray times. That trail was smaller. Why does your glance rest on the dip in the meadow, on the scar in the trunk of the fir tree, the armless faun, Mademoiselle de Fauche? Do you still see the traces left by the occupation? You say to me "What a shame! A king would not have allowed this!" That France was not at the pinnacle her past had attained? Perhaps . . .

Do you hear those birds? Did they also sing amid the stench of diesel fuel and the noise of military vehicles? They are everywhere, do you see them? That one can't maneuver for all the trees. You tell me they were officers, gave no cause for complaints, behaved like gentlemen. Yes, you billeted more than eighty of them; you had no choice.

Were they also gentlemen, those Germans who deported the Jewish children from Montintin, hanged hostages on the main square, sent my aunt Rosi to Auschwitz, ruined Lizzi's life? For two years, Rudi Lepkowitz hid in a wall closet! And you didn't even lose your virginity, Mademoiselle de Fauche!

"Je ne me suis jamais mariée, Monsieur . . . Mes frères . . . Vous savez . . ."

I knew it. Being married would have meant living in the present. You preferred to let the past accumulate, pile up, tied into orderly bundles, so that you might draw on this supply, live on experiences of the past.

Therefore my pilgrimage into your domain, Mademoiselle de Fauche. That's why I'm here, in your manor house, thirty-nine years later. You knew me when I was a child. You remember me. What was I like? Tell me, Mademoiselle de Fauche. What was I like? Could one read in my face that I was aware of what was going on?

The late afternoon revives the charm of the house, uses a pale red to paint the faded walls, slate, closed shutters, crumbled bricks, buttresses, black chimneys. The tin weathervane displays its rust. There is the annex where we lived. Yellow. I couldn't remember that it had a color. The latrine must be behind those bushes, farther back the cherry trees. This German shepherd, why is it barking like that? I'm glad it is kept on a chain. My Toutou wasn't that wild. Strange little dog . . . He brought us eggs, one after the other.

Where did he steal them? How did he know that we needed them so badly? One day Toutou brought the hen, and he had to be killed. The *maître* shot him dead. That happened shortly before our departure.

"Je me souviens très bien de vous, Monsieur . . . Vous aviez à peu près douze ans . . . Vous habitez au Mexique, maintenant? . . . Ah, les Toltèques, Monsieur . . . un grand peuple . . ."

Yes, we escaped just in time. Even though an armistice had been signed, the Gestapo had a foothold in "free" France, and the Jews were trapped. Pau. The Pyrenees. Winter. "Napoléon Troisième était un imbécile, Monsieur . . . Vous ne croyez pas? Si les Espagnols . . ." If the Spaniards had opened the border, how many of the persecuted could have been saved! How often we tried to reach Spain in order to get from there to Lisbon before we finally succeeded on the last day of 1941. I can't remember. Did you ever see a father who in his despair smokes newsprint, Mademoiselle de Fauche? That was the day they opened the border – perhaps only for a few days – and by chance we were there. We were lucky. "La France a manqué d'un mouvement de réaction national, ouioui Monsieur . . . Si Pétain . . ."

I like your "ouiouis" that you slurp up as if to draw breath from your statements. You needn't strain your memory, Mademoiselle de Fauche. Strange to see your face light up with all these memories. It's true: we did live with Klara and Walter Grün. "Les valeurs de l'esprit français, Monsieur . . ." Oh yes, Mademoiselle. You had cheap labor when you hired Walter and my father as gardeners.

"Votre père jouait du violon . . ."

Did he? I can't remember. He had his fiddle, true, and perhaps he did play occasionally.

"Des valses viennoises . . ."

How easy it was for you to draw them into the present. Something I can't do. Why not? Help me, Mademoiselle de Fauche! What were we like? What do I care that France had lost faith in herself! Quit digressing! My mother, what was she like? How? Did she smile at times? Yes, Klara Grün had been a medical student in Vienna. You remember everything. Like us, she fled to Paris in 1938. Then to the South of France. She died in Mexico. "Maximilian c'est proclamé empéreur des Aztèques, parce que

Napoléon Troisième..."

We enter the only unlocked room. You've reduced your living space in order to simplify your life, Mademoiselle de Fauche. You've locked doors, covered the many memories with linen cloths.

The sun gradually withdraws from the room. Geraniums, framed by the door, in brightest bloom. The old lady makes tea. I don't tire of watching how memories prop up her ninety-three years. Sepia family pictures remain in semi-darkness, a daguerreotype – children in front of a school – is briefly illuminated.

A whistle... Monsieur Bigère... Is he still alive? I, we run into the classroom, "slow-ly, do-not-run, no rea-son-to-hurry, children," second row, my seat. Creaky desks. Shuffling shoes. The chalk dust in the air trembles from the chorus of "Allons, enfants de la patriiie..." As I stand by my desk, singing, I see the fleur-de-lis-framed portrait of one of the Fauches fading in the twilight. I try to shake chestnuts from the trees over there, to hit the big marble, to stuff my pockets with them, to outdo my brother in soccer. Go on playing, never stop playing. I do not want to go home, to have to memorize those hated summaries, and there is nothing to eat but nettles and Jerusalem artichokes, garnished with a bad mood.

How could it happen that I lost those hundred francs when I went into town to buy bread? I don't know, Papa... I just lost that one bill. How much was one hundred francs? "Ah, le Mexique des Aztèques, Monsieur..." What did one hundred francs buy? One loaf of bread? Twenty? Once the woman in the bakery smiled at me and didn't require food coupons. When I went to see you yesterday, madame la boulangère, there you were, gray-haired, wearing glasses. Forgive me, I didn't have the courage to thank you. Returning makes my tears well up easily.

"Vous alliez partout a vélo... ouioui... je me souviens très bien..."

My wooden bicycle! It squeals as I speed down the Route Albi at top speed... How fresh the air is in spite of all my anxieties! Step on the pedals! "Douce France, souvenir de mon enfance..." To the river, catching catfish!... Spitting off the bridge!... Then herding old man Massip's sheep, for food and a liter of milk...

Mademoiselle de Fauche, 93 years old, in 1981

Stealing grapes in Beausoleil... the good ones, wrapped in paper... One has to avoid farms with geese . . . Later, going swimming, comparing dicks and butts . . . Collecting mussels in the Tescou . . . "Douce France sans couleur, souvenir de mon enfance . . ." Tra-la-la, la . . . Going home! It's late . . . The bridge . . . And then up the hill . . . How steep that trail is! . . . Step on it, boy! . . . The tall iron gate . . . The Park, gray and mysterious . . . The gloomy manor house . . . And there you are, Mademoiselle. In black-and-white, exactly as you are thirty-nine years later. Take a good look at me. I will be your memory! . . . There is Mama . . . Is she in color? Look at what I am looking at, and answer me: Is there blue, green? Is the shit in the latrine brown?

The sun stipples have already vanished from the room. "A king would not have permitted this, Monsieur." The old woman pulls her shawl closer around her. It is cool. "What a shame. France was not at the pinnacle of her past." Like a chameleon she blends into her environs.

I say farewell to you, Mademoiselle de Fauche. I don't reproach you for anything. I don't even blame you for living off my experiences.

If there is no past left for you to hoard, then it's your turn to stow yourself away in your collection of memories.

Chapter 13

FLEEING TO LISBON

It's a distance of about three hours from Montauban to Pau. We checked into a run-down hotel in the center of town, intending to take the first available train to Canfranc, the border station high in the Pyrenees. While we waited for the opportunity to book seats on one of the twice-daily trains, we strolled from bench to bench in the city parks. We ate the heads of geese one could buy for close to nothing at one of the grill booths. Yes, we had to save for the trip. I remember an almost translucent atmosphere with a great deal of sun, which gave us a clear view of the mountains we were trying to cross. They warned us that Gestapo agents were in town.

The events of those days deepened the gaps in my memory. My mother and my brother told me later that we went up to Canfranc several times and were turned back by the border guards, both the Spaniards and the French. But I have no recollection of these trips. So what! The fact is they didn't let us pass and we had to return to Pau.

It is quite possible that the attack on Pearl Harbor and the American entry into the World War three weeks earlier had influenced the border closings. It may also be that an over-eager official thought he had discovered irregularities in our documents or simply wanted to be difficult. I don't know and was never able to get to the bottom of this.

Our situation was critical since we had to enter Portugal no later than January 1, or the visa issued in Marseille would expire. So we had to renew it at the last possible minute. There was no way for us to make it to Portugal in time, even if we got through Canfranc on December 31. My father was so desperate that he secretly picked up cigarette butts off the street, rolled the tobacco in a piece of newspaper, and smoked it. At last, on December 30 at the Portuguese Consulate in Pau, he was given the indispensable stamp to renew the visa, surprisingly enough one without an expiration date. Did that mean that January 1, as indicated on the Marseille visa, was still applicable?

The next day we took that train once more. We arrived in Canfranc late in the afternoon. It was very cold in the large halls of the station. Again we had difficulties with the officials. I never knew what kind; Helmut did not remember either. He helped Papa, who spoke very little French, in these discussions, or maybe he just hoped that they would listen to his pleas. We waited anxiously. Did I cry? Perhaps I did. At last the miracle happened. We were ordered to the platform where a locomotive and a few cars were ready for departure. It was evening by the time we went aboard. After a few more fearful minutes of delay, the train started to move.

What had happened? Why did they let us pass this time? A change of policy on the Spanish side? Did we encounter a compassionate official or one with leftist sympathies, as happened to the Papaneks at the border control in Cerbère? I don't know.

I decided in 1997 to cross the border at the same place one more time. From Montauban, I went to Pau with the firm intention of taking the train up into the mountains to Canfranc. But that train connection had been discontinued in the 1970s, and I had to take a bus. There were only a few passengers. To have a good view, I sat in the first row. The road ran nearly parallel to the tracks. The sight of the mountains was overwhelming, but even more impressive were the rails, eerie, rusted! How many hopeful refugees must have traveled on them! The viaducts and the large number of tunnels into which the rails disappeared, twenty-four, to be exact, revived in me the impression I had of this journey as a child. At some moments, I felt again the shaking, groaning and howling of the locomotive, the intervals of darkness as we passed through the tunnels. And the fear.

The sight of the Canfranc station was baffling. The area was completely abandoned and desolate, a tangle of rails, overgrown with weeds. Inside the station – seventy years ago one of the largest in Europe, an architectural jewel in the neoclassical style, over seven hundred feet long – only a single small hall was still occupied to clear the two daily trains leaving for Zaragoza. The futuristic project of establishing a direct link between Paris and Madrid had ended in failure.

I walked slowly through the outer passageways with their remnants of art-nouveau decorations and tried to peer through the dirty windows. I could recognize immigration and customs offices, identified on still legible signs in French and Spanish, and the hall with the benches where fifty-six years ago we had waited, stiff with tension. Then there was a loud roar and two young German motorcyclists who were exploring the area as tourists showed up. When I told them that I had passed through here during the war to save my life, they had a hard time understanding what I was talking about. I climbed into the first-class car and reclined in my seat, absorbed in memories.

On that January1, 1942 we stood all the way to Zaragoza, the car fully occupied by soldiers. The cold winter air from the high mountains came in through the broken windows. I squatted down in a corner between two cars and paid attention to what was going on around me. I fell asleep. In Zaragoza we transferred to the Madrid train. It too was full. Our time of arrival in Madrid was important because my father was worried about getting to Portugal in time. I don't know for sure when we managed to get on a train to Lisbon, but it probably was the same midnight train that I took when I repeated the trip in 1997. In the turmoil at the station, one of our suitcases was stolen.

Today I am sure that we were traveling late at night since I can remember my amazement when at dawn I saw the extensive olive groves on the peninsula. Besides that, the stamp in our travel documents shows that we left Spain at Valencia de Alcántara on January 2, which indicates that the visa issued in Pau was the valid one. Or it was a sign of fate that we were saved despite the mistake of a border official who could not, or perhaps would not, add thirty days to the date of December 3.

At the station in Lisbon, we were welcomed with tears and embraces, many embraces. Friends of my father, Max Diamant, a German Social Democrat, foremost among them and like us

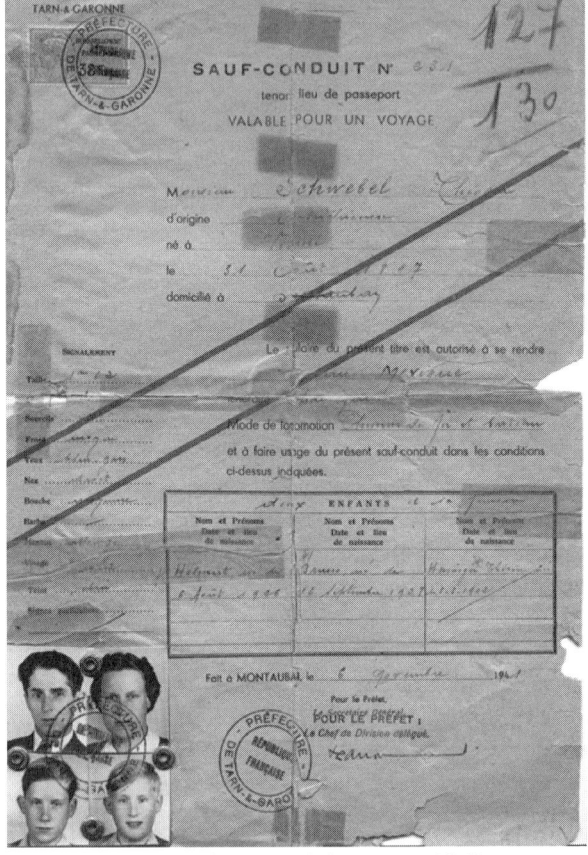
Section of our travel document, 1941

emigrating to Mexico, put us up in a boarding house, the "Residencia Roma," half a block from the Avenida da Liberdade. What an appropriate name!

The first thing my father did was to retrieve a twenty-dollar bill he had hidden in a shoe heel. The bill was completely tattered but Papa, with help from his friends, was able to exchange it for escudos. His next step was to run to a bakery and buy a bag of bolos (cakes). We celebrated in our room, telling jokes and laughing. We hadn't laughed for a long time.

Lisbon exuded a calmness and warmth, a balm to mind and

body. Every morning vendors with baskets full of fish came through the streets offering their wares. I can still hear them shouting "Peixe . . .! peixe fresco!" under our second-floor window. Since my father had to deal with the final formalities of our journey to Mexico, my brother and I explored the historic center of town or went to the Caìs das Colunas (Pier of Columns) where the *Nyassa* was anchored, the ship aboard which we would soon be sailing. On a Sunday we crossed the Tejo in a boat to get to the Costa da Caparica. For the first time in my life, I saw the ocean. The salty wind, the shrieks of the gulls, the thundering of the breakers at the beach fascinated me in a way that would hold me in their grip my whole life.

During my visit to Lisbon in 1997, something happened that would often recur during this entire journey into the past. Slowly those impressions I had taken in fifty-six years ago came back to me: the streetcar that, with its bell ringing, rattled through the narrow streets, my inability to understand the language, the insistent taste of the *bacalhao*, the painful smallpox vaccination that was required for boarding the *Nyassa*. Strolling past a *livraria*, I remembered the book *Mis primeros pinitos en el castellano*, a present and my introduction to Spanish. Where might I have lost it? Reenacting a stroll I had taken as a boy with my brother, I walked through the Rua Aogusta toward the pier. Only tourist boats and luxury yachts were lying at anchor. The big ships were somewhere else, far from here.

Every day Helmut and I were in a hurry to get to the Cais so we could observe the preparations for the *Nyassa's* departure. Never before had we seen a ship like this, four hundred feet long and then some. The ones on the Danube had been much, much smaller. She had an impressive smoke stack and equally impressive bow and stern masts that were connected with a long hawser. With all those flags, she reminded me of a gigantic clotheshorse. Would there be enough lifeboats for all those passengers? A few yards above the water line, the bull's-eyes of the cabins were looking at us. Would I soon be looking through one of them? The size of the two bow anchors was a sight to see. Future passengers always came to the pier, all of them with anticipation in their eyes. We became friends

Section of our travel document showing the visa for Mexico, top right, signed on November 6, 1941, by the Mexican Consul General in Marseille, Gilberto Bosques

with some of these people, exchanged a buenos días or a remark about where we were from, about the beauty of the city and the delay of the ship's departure. That was my first approach to the Spanish language.

On the morning of January 28, 1942, hanging onto our suitcases, we joined the long line of those about to board the *Nyassa*.

Chapter 14

THE CROSSING

The Nyassa was an old 9000-ton freighter, built in Bremen at the beginning of the century and later refurbished to transport about 2000 passengers. In that capacity, she had been sailing under a Portuguese flag, making many voyages to take emigrants to the ports of Latin America, the United States, Palestine, and other destinations. The bunks of third-class passengers, meaning people like us, were located in her huge cargo holds, with separate quarters for women and men. It was a gloomy and damp place, crowded with berths, one on top of the other. My brother had been assigned a bed on the "upper floor," I and all others who were prone to get seasick bedded down on the ground floor. That way we were less likely to soil somebody when we threw up.

All passengers had come on deck so they could experience the ship's departure down the Tejo. I had secured a spot up front where I was able to watch the mighty bowsprit cut through the waves and drag long stripes of foam along the ship's hull. This image impressed itself on my memory more deeply than any other sight. The sea was calm and the slow up-and-down didn't bother me much as long as I was distracted by the shrieking gulls which were following the ship, by the receding coastline and the fishing boats, by the view of Lisbon's southern districts which gradually disappeared in the morning's mist. Dolphins emerged several times ahead and alongside of us as if to guide the *Nyassa* out into the open sea. I was very excited, thinking they were sharks. That was before Flipper had become part of a child's world. "Look, dolphins!" people kept saying until both the seagulls and the dolphins were harder and harder to spot as we left the coast farther and farther behind. The need to vomit started instead.

I was seasick the entire voyage. Clinging to the rail, I threw up into the Atlantic before the Cabo de Sao Vicente, then along the coast of Morocco. My only consolation was that any number of people were going through the same misery. All around me, they were throwing up in German, Spanish, Catalan, Yiddish, and who knows in how many other languages. In Casablanca – the *Nyassa* lay calmly at anchor – I spent a part of the time barfing into the completely motionless sea. Aside from the surfeit of sun and the staccato shouts of the Arabic stevedores, this is my only memory of our brief stopover. We were not permitted to go ashore, a disappointment I try to compensate for these days by watching *Casablanca* (with Humphrey Bogart and Ingrid Bergmann) or *Pépé le Moko* (with Jean Gabin) as often as possible. I observed the large crowd of passengers boarding, most of whom had left Marseille by different routes, a long line of hopeful faces.

The *Nyassa* was scheduled to sail from Lisbon by way of Casablanca, the Bermudas, Havana, Veracruz, and Santo Domingo. There were approximately 2500 passengers on board, which exceeded the designated maximum by far. There were so many rats that infants had to be watched day and night to prevent a disaster. During a similar passage on the St. Tomé, my newborn cousin, Peter, was saved from the rats by Brígida Alexander, who was pregnant with her twins, Susana and Beto, and was traveling with her husband, the engineer Katz, and her son, Didier. Some of the passengers on our ship, Walter Grün for one, had to make do with the least amount of space, far down below in the ship's entrails, near the stables and convicts. Others among our fellow travelers were Käthe Bodek with her sons (Klaus and Uli), Klari Willner, Paul Westheim (I believe), the anthropologist Laurette Séjourné, Gertrude Kurz, Arnaldo Orfila, who was later to start the publishing companies Fondo de Cultura Económica and Siglo XXI, as well as other people I was to become acquainted with later in Mexico.

Most of the passengers were Spanish Republicans. Since the ocean was very rough, it was not often that we could gather round the young people who were singing and dancing on the decks, the music of guitars and castanets carrying everywhere. Helmut and I became friends with three sisters, Manola, Cármen, and Pilar. Later, in Mexico, my brother often went to meet Pilar at the Colegio Luis Vives, the school preferred by the Spanish Republicans. They became good school friends. When the sea was heavy, everyone withdrew into their cabins or lined up in front of the toilets to vomit. My mother did all she could to alleviate my constant nausea. Why did it take so long for Dramamine, a medication against seasickness, to reach the market? The only thing that helped was to get out into the open air, a dangerous venture on account of the poor weather. One could enter certain areas of the decks only while wearing a life vest, which is why I was resigned to suffering in my bunk. These were times when Mexico occupied my imagination.

I had not the slightest idea what to expect. In this regard, I must have felt like one of the great discoverers, with expectations that may not have been much different than those of a Cortés or of the first Vikings in America. Notions of pistols, of horses and Indians with huge hats had captivated me, which was about the extent of what most Europeans with very little exposure to cultures on another continent knew. I remember my mother getting a letter from a Hössinger relative with a warning to watch out for Indians lurking in the jungle.

Whenever I try to picture the dining room of the *Nyassa* in my memory, the images I see overlap with those excerpts from the Chaplin movie *The Immigrant*, where the plates on the table slide back and forth in harmony with the motion of the reeling ship. In our case, even the silverware frequently changed owners. The meals, consisting mostly of salted cod and sardines, were much too greasy for Austrian stomachs. And what little didn't come up again was hard to digest. But tea was served generously. "Mais chá?" was the crew's routine question.

The voyage to the Bermudas took more than two weeks. It was a worrisome time, most of it spent on a turbulent ocean. One morning a periscope appeared in the distance. A German submarine? We never found out. Would the U-boats of the Wolf Pack respect the flag of neutral Portugal? The *Nyassa* had turned on all her lights so as not to be mistaken for a warship. I remember that all of us pushed toward starboard, pointing the periscope out. There was good reason to be fearful because German actions were unpredictable, especially in view of the sinking, in September 1939, of the English ship S. S. *Athenia*, with more than a thousand civilians on board. The majority of them fortunately survived. After the worldwide indignation caused by the attack, Hitler is said to have given orders to his U-boat fleet no longer to attack passenger ships. But all the same, the Germans sank the *Champlain* and H. M. S. *Carinthia* in June 1940, in July of that year the *Arandora Star*, and in October the *Empress of Britain*. In September 1942 the *Monte Corbea* met her fate, in October the *Duchess of Atholl*, and in December the *Ceramic*, 1943 the *Serpa Pinto* and, I'm sure, a few more.

These events were some of the many issues at the Nuremberg Trial in 1946 when Admiral Dönitz was sentenced to ten years in prison for crimes against humanity.

For us, the Bermuda Islands were not the paradise so praised by international tourism these days. For a few days, we had passed through severe storms, and bad weather accompanied us to Hamilton, the capital city. Today, when I think of the soot-covered figures who emerged from the belly of the *Nyassa* while they were loading coal, I am reminded of B. Traven's *The Death Ship*. Who were the people who spent days and even weeks down in the bowels of the ship to stoke the boilers. Portuguese? Refugees wandering about from border to border with entry refused, as the novel describes? Perhaps. The ship was surrounded by swarms of sardines and several of the passengers tried to fish, surely to take their minds off other things. At night the *Nyassa's* lights were extinguished so as not to draw attention to the presence of American warships.

Klaus Bodek – in the memoirs he wrote for Steven Spielberg's *Project Shoah* – and Walter Grün reminded me of a tragic accident. The son of a passenger named Theissen was killed when he fell into one of the open hatches while playing with other boys. His family and a few friends who constituted the required *minyan* buried him on the island in a hurry.

I don't know the reason, perhaps because the *Nyassa* could not take up enough coal, but the fact is that when she weighed anchor, we were told that she would call at Norfolk, Virginia. All of us were moved by the announcement that we were coming so close to the United States, the country to which so many had wanted to emigrate. It was of great importance to all of us to see the port with what certainly would be magnificent installations. It was an ambivalent feeling to see but not be able to enter a longed-for and yet inaccessible land.

As we passed Cape Henry and entered the Bay of Norfolk, the base of the Atlantic Fleet, we boys were fascinated by the multitude of warships, gigantic, gray, their steel glistening in the light rain, cannons and American flags everywhere. The port was heavily guarded and protected since a short time earlier U-boats of the Wolf Pack had sneaked in and sunk two ships. I had no doubt that this heavily equipped navy was meant, sooner or later, to take on the German fleet. The piers were teeming with naval police, all of them armed to the teeth and keeping an eye on everything. The loading was done with great precision while we admired the coordinated utilization of cranes.

A few days later, the *Nyassa* berthed at the piers of Havana. Here too we were not permitted to go ashore. And here I experienced tropical heat for the first time. Vendors of all stripes were trying to do business from the quay. Sums of money were negotiated loudly; some of the passengers hauled up pineapples, bananas, and other tropical fruit in baskets and sent down money, dollars, I presume. A relaxed atmosphere, full of laughter and joshing, dickering in sign language, quite in contrast to gray, warlike Norfolk. Such a world would surely await us in Veracruz too. From our deck, we watched the blinking signals of the lighthouse El Moro and the bustle on El Malecón. We could see many bicycles and pushcarts and many dark-skinned people. My nausea had abated and I was able to join in the noise and dancing of the young people on the quarterdeck. The next morning, the *Nyassa* pushed off in a westerly direction in order to cross the Gulf of Mexico. At last, after five weeks at sea, we heard someone shout: "Veracruz ahead!" It was night and indeed, one could spot the lights of the port in the distance. The engines were stopped. The sea was very calm, in contrast to our nerves. The *Nyassa* laid to. Shortly thereafter, a strong wind with rain came up, my first *norte* in Mexico. Next morning we entered the port. From the entrance into the bay we saw the pier, crowded with waving people. As we got closer, we heard the shouts more clearly and the typical mariachi and jarocho musicians. Our reception was unforgettable. People were trying to recognize relatives or friends and send welcoming shouts their way. Never before had I experienced that much contagious weeping. But we passengers had not been given permission as yet to go ashore. Were there problems with the authorities? A repetition of the *St. Louis* tragedy? It took another day before we were allowed to disembark. We were greeted by representatives of various aid organizations. No difficulties with the formalities. One more stamp was added to our travel document: "Secretaría de Gobernación. México. Asilado político. 3 de Marzo de 1942."

Chapter 15

MEXICO, THE FIRST WEEKS

March 3, the day we went ashore, was Mama's fortieth birthday and also her wedding anniversary. Yes, my parents started their new life in Mexico and their nineteenth year of marriage at the same time.

Together with other German-speaking refugees, we were taken to the capital city on a bus the welcoming committee had rented. Someone in our group compared our arrival with that of a different party of Austrians who had landed here seventy-eight years ago. He mentioned that the Emperor Maximilian had been received less cordially and, to make things worse, had been obliged to spend the night on a billiard table, tortured by mosquitoes. But perhaps I was much too captivated by the new impressions to think about who that compatriot might have been and what he was doing in Mexico.

We set out rather late in the morning. I have only a very vague recollection of the drive through town, remembering only the large number of potholes. After a short while, the view broadened and we saw wide meadows, banana plantations, mango trees with an incredibly dense profusion of leaves, herds of zebu cattle with their entourage of herons. I'd like to believe that my love of the countryside around Veracruz, which would stay with me for the rest of my life, arose from these first impressions. Everybody's eyes were glued to the window panes of the bus. In Jalapa, I believe, we stopped to get something to drink and to taste one of the regional snacks – my first encounter with hot Mexican chili. Here I heard for the first time, and I'm sure was very impressed, that the Emperor Moctezuma had been served fresh fish every day. Aztec runners carried it from the coast to Tenochtitlán, a distance of 250 miles.

Contrary to Mama's fear, I didn't get sick as we drove on a road with a seemingly unending number of curves. The view of Pico de Orizaba, the continuous chain of villages, chasms, and precipices and thinking about the Aztec runners occupied me more than enough. And Maximilian – did he travel by coach or perhaps ride a mule? I remember being very impressed by the dust devils that rise in the highlands before Puebla during the dry season. In the twilight, we were able to see the grandiose silhouette of Mt. Popocatépetl. Someone shouted: "Big Poopy!" and amused all of us with his infectious laughter. We were in a good mood, very close to our destination.

Driving into the capital at night through the crowded quarters of Candelaria and Morelos with their obvious poverty made a very strong impression on me. Was this the city where we would live? Our arrival at the Hotel Vizcaya on the Calle Peru intensified my disappointment even further. We and a few others of our group got off here, attentively watched by a number of prostitutes. Our welcome was friendly words from Dr. Ernst Frenk, at that time the husband of the celebrated author Marianne Frenk-Westheim and the grandfather of the present-day Secretary of Health, Julio Frenk. The other travelers were taken to equally cheap hotels in the city.

The Vizcaya still exists, though now in a state of restoration. It is located near the Mercado de la Lagunilla, six or seven blocks from the center of town and two from the Arena Coliseo, a venue for boxing and freestyle wrestling. Years later, when I was training at the engineering school for wrestling contests, I was tempted to accept an offer to turn professional. They even had picked a ring name for me: "Babyface!" These days the arena has lost some of its aggressive atmosphere and even the prostitutes are no longer as impudent as they were back then.

We four Schwebels were put up in a spacious room with two wide beds (which the hotel reserved for orgies?). Once we had become settled, we devoted ourselves to reconnoitering the district from our window. It was our first confrontation with the used-clothes vendors, the shrill whistle of the steam from the *camote* vendors' fake locomotives, the beggars, the organ grinders, the *pepenadores*, the sisters of Mercy, the whores and their pimps, the drunks on the sidewalks. It was my first contact with the cooking stalls in the streets, the dirt, the traffic, the shouts of the lottery vendors, and the music turned on at full blast. And at the hotel's reception desk, I had my first exposure to the native language: *güerito* (Blondie) here and *güerito* there.

It must have been an extraordinary occurrence at the hotel that a group of foreigners showed up who were neither gringos nor tourists. My brother and I were the cause of constant giggling and whispering. What did these two tall boys in short pants want if they did not respond to seductive invitations like: "Come here, *güerito*, I'll show you something" but looked like they were from another planet. I'm sure we must have seemed strange, as strange as the activities of the girls looked to me when they disappeared, snuggling into their companions' arms, into the rooms. Through a barely covered window Helmut and I, with eyes wide open, saw a couple making love. Yes, Mexico did welcome my curiosity about all things sexual.

An organization of liberal Jews, all of them Social Democrats and known as the "Bundists," together with friends who had arrived in Mexico before us, among them Phillip Müller and Resi Mandl, looked after us during the first weeks. I recall a dinner at a restaurant, the tables decorated with red carnations, during which there was no lack of welcoming speeches and expressions of gratitude.

On our first strolls through the city center, I was reminded of the streets in Lisbon: the old buildings with their cast-iron balcony rails and geranium pots, the shrieking of the streetcars as they rounded corners, busses with crowds of passengers, beggars, shoeshine boys. A language I didn't understand, strange facial features. I'm sure I had expected to find Indians like those described in Karl May's stories. In great amazement, I walked by the delicatessen and confectionary shops, the cafés with the strong aroma of coffee and cigarettes, crowded with people engaged in discussions and reading newspapers. And every time I passed by the Salón Cervecería Modelo on the Calle de Allende, forever my restaurant of choice to eat tacos and wash them down with a tall lager, I was without fail pulled in by the spicy scent of chorizo.

The restaurant where we ate was the Fornos on Calle Bolívar, very close to the corner of Calle Venustiano Carranza, and it is here

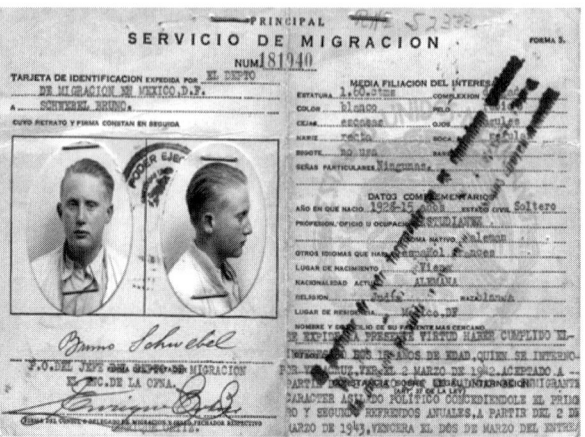
My first identification card as a political refugee, "Asilado Politico," Mexico 1943

that I had my first lessons in Mexican Spanish. At breakfast we tried to identify the little sweet rolls with such exotic names as *chilindrinas, ojos de pancha* (girls' eyes), *regañadas, piedras* (stones) or *pan de nalga* (buttock bread), an exercise much more instructive than the booklet *Mis primeros pinitos en el castellano* we had been given in Lisbon. Perhaps this *pan de nalga*, which isn't made any longer, gave one of the waiters an opportunity to kid me with a typical Mexican play on words (*albur*). At the Fornos I discovered my preference for *huevos rancheros* (fried eggs on tortillas with chili sauce), for the warm *bolillos* (rolls) and fresh-squeezed orange juice. At lunchtime I learned about *comida corrida*, consisting of *sopa aguada* ("liquid" soup), *sopa seca* (dry soup), an entrée, black beans, a very, very sweet dessert, and tasteless coffee, served in a large cup with as much sugar as one wanted.

While my parents looked around to find a place to live, my brother and I took off, every day straying a little farther away from the hotel. Calle del Órgano and Dos de Abril, with their whores sitting in front of doorless rooms with their legs spread wide apart, were areas we observed only from afar. Music was drawing us toward the Plaza Garibaldi, where mariachis were vying loudly for customers, the night owls were whooping their "jijajai!," and the drunkards were staggering through the crowd. This square amazes me to this day, how much must it have impressed me as a child! I remember that, mesmerized by the staccato rhythm of "La Culebra" (the Snake), I gawked at the *charro* suits of the musicians, the size of the *guitarrones*, the singers with long hair, scratchy voices, and deep décolletages. Soon our excursions took us all the way to Alameda Park. The photographers probably didn't get us to ride one of the wooden horses, but I'm very sure we would have wanted to taste the *churros* (sweet breadsticks), *buñuelos* (puff pastries), *alegrías* (hard cakes made of amaranth and lots of sugar), and colorfully decorated wafers. We ogled the girls in their tight-fitting dresses and the kissing couples. One day we went to the zoo of Chapultepec, a visit whose highlight was a masturbating monkey. Given all these sensual seductions, my first strands of pubic hair started to sprout, and so two weeks of Mexico was all I needed to complete my theoretical knowledge of sexuality. All that was missing was the practical part. But that would take a few more years.

A short time later, we moved to a dark and squalid three-room apartment on Calle Tlaxcala. It was one of those typical tenement houses that exist to this day: about twenty apartments on three floors, grouped around an oblong inner court. Rent amounted to twenty-five pesos per month. The very first thing we did was scrub the floors with steel wool and clean up the kitchen for Mama. Somebody brought us mattresses, and in the corners of the rooms we improvised closets by hanging up old drapes in order to stow our few belongings. In the center of the courtyard was a telephone for all residents, jealously guarded by the super, a fat man with gloomy eyes. The number was Mexicana P-90-50. I don't know why it still sticks to my mind. It may have been my anchor in this gigantic city, and that is perhaps the reason my brain refuses to erase it from my memory even sixty years later.

We lived half a block off the Avenida de los Insurgentes, but for all that it was a quiet neighborhood with many trees and little traffic, so quiet and low traffic in fact that we were awakened in the morning by roosters crowing on the flat roofs and at Christmas by the natives walking by with flocks of *pípilas* (turkeys). A streetcar ran back and forth on the Avenida de los Insurgentes, crossing the Avenida Baja California, and then turning near the Glorieta de

Chilpancingo to return to the city center. Everything beyond that was terra incognita. To take a ride to Coyoacán in order to stroll along the Calle Francisco Sosa or to go to San Ángel to marvel at the hand of General Obregon in its glass case were excursion plans we had to postpone until later. There was grass growing between the streetcar tracks, and I think I remember seeing a herd of sheep grazing there; well, perhaps it was just one sheep. It is quite possible that I've retained too idyllic a picture of this area. But chickens there were for sure. They belonged to a Greek woman, a heavy-set person who spoke faulty Spanish and ran a store by the name she was called, la Griega. Her chickens had learned how to survive the passing streetcars and the red ramshackle, exhaust-spewing busses. The birds hectically flapping their wings always were a cause of laughter and amazement. Nothing of all this has survived. What has remained is a district overcrowded with people, stores, movie theaters, booming music, and garbage.

We lived a few minutes away from Parque México. On Sundays the park would be full of sauntering people, sometimes an orchestra played golden oldies, and in the afternoon one could hear the spectators in the nearby bullfight arena shouting their "Olés." This is where ten years later I made my debut as a television camera man, to the despair of the producer mistaking the matadors for the *monosabios*.

These days only a few nags pulling little carts for children are left of what in Don Porfirio Diaz's time was a race track, and only a few beautiful houses and a traffic circle bearing her name remind one of the aristocratic atmosphere associated with the Countess of Miravalle, the former owner of this whole area. On Saturdays it is Jews wearing yarmulkes who go for walks there.

Even though my brother and I didn't wear yarmulkes, it was at that time that one of the few anti-Semitic insults we ever heard was aimed at us. There was a gang that called itself "del Parras," whose members chased us a few times with shouts like "pinches judíos" (dirty kikes). We were a little afraid, obviously, but far less so than during the persecutions in Purkersdorf. One day I stood up to one of them and then to another one; we bloodied each other's noses and after that they left us alone. My brother, who at that time was taller and stronger than I, had the reputation of a good fighter, which is why they provoked him more often than me.

But our real contact with Mexico didn't start until we went to school. We hadn't been living on Calle Tlaxcala for long when our parents decided to enroll us in a public school. The most suitable one was the Escuela Prevocacional No. 2 of the Polytechnic Institute in Tacubaya, about fifteen minutes from our house. The school was located on the Calle Benjamin Hill in an old building with a courtyard, previously used as a shoe factory and directly across from the German Alexander von Humboldt School. When my brother and I showed up there, hair neatly combed, in short pants and unable to speak Spanish, the registrar, Señor Argudin, explained to us in a friendly voice that we had made a mistake: the German school was across the street. It took some effort but we managed to inform him of our situation, and even though classes had started two months earlier we were allowed to register.

The principal, Ernesto Verdugo, alias El Pirata – he limped and wore dark glasses – was a kind man who treated everybody, but especially the two of us, with courtesy. The ritual for newcomers was to have their heads shaved, a procedure performed by the wildest kids in third grade. So on the second day, before classes, we found ourselves surrounded by boys armed with scissors. I started thinking about past attacks and got scared but didn't try to run away. They had a hard time with Helmut who fought back like a ram about to be shorn, but half of my hair was cut off. In view of this fuss, the registrar gave orders to leave us be. But we didn't want to give the impression that we were claiming special privileges, and so we decided to have a barber give us a total haircut. Oh yes, we also bought long pants to avoid being constantly whistled at.

What a difference between that environment and the discipline in the Austrian and French schools! I felt it necessary to adapt to these circumstances and become one of those boys who were so very different from me, some already wearing a mustache, close to manhood. At the same time, I had been shaped by European patterns of behavior. This difference stayed with me for the rest of my life in Mexico.

It did not take long for our vocabulary to increase. "*Chingar*," a popular Mexican swear word and its derivations, quickly became one of my most frequently used expressions, but obviously the manifold variants of the word "*madre*" required more time. We learned in a hurry what a "*guamazo*" (punch) was, or what "*te quieres dar?*" (want to fight?) meant, and a challenging look was answered with "*habas, güey*!", the precise sense of which is puzzling to me even now. Indeed, first basic lessons for life.

In the middle of May, Uncle Oskar and Aunt Anni arrived with their five children: Dita (16), Herbert (13 and 1/2, like me), Nelly (10), Alfons (5), and Peter, less than one year old. They also moved into an apartment in the tenement house on Calle Tlaxcala. The flight from Austria and the dissemination of their Schwebel genes could become – I have not the slightest doubt about this – the material for a soap opera of epic proportions.

My father started looking for work: to give violin lessons or to join an orchestra and become the first Viennese mariachi? Because of his small size and his black hair he wouldn't have been very conspicuous, especially if he had also grown a mustache. But first he had to learn Spanish. An interim solution was the door-to-door sale of sausages to customers whose addresses he obtained from the Asociación de Judíos Askenazi. He carried his goods in a large briefcase. In the evening, he told us about his stammering in Spanish, about haggling with difficult clients, and about the problems that arose because he smelled like Hungarian salami. Often he found himself circled by alley mutts who pursued him until he took refuge in the streetcar. He decided to switch from sausages to chocolate, which wasn't much of a success either, since his merchandise had a tendency to melt on hot days. But despite all these commercial failures, he never lost his positive attitude. Once he told us that, while climbing on to the streetcar, he set his briefcase on the floor bell of the rear platform, much to the amusement of the passengers and to the chagrin of the driver.

My mother started to sew wedding dresses, with help from her sister-in-law, Anni. Their pay was miserable. To expose this type of exploitation had been the reason for joining in the work of the

Social Democrats during their years in Neulengbach.

A few weeks later, my father received a small loan from his sister, Dora, whose family had settled in the United States, and an additional loan from Israelite organizations. This financial support enabled him to take over a small grocery store on Calle de Allende, around the corner from the Hotel Vizcaya. His regular customers were the Jews who had started their businesses a considerable time ago in the center of the city, especially in streets like Jesús María, del Carmen, República de Cuba, and others in nearby districts. He also perfected his Yiddish and, a Spanish dictionary at hand, he settled down in La Lagunilla. Poor Papa. All his political commitments in Austria were of no use in Mexico; his violin rested forgotten in a corner.

About fifteen years ago – my father had died by then – I sold his beloved violin. It was a good instrument, not especially valuable but in tolerable condition. Only the case showed signs of serious damage as if the traces of those difficult years had been imprinted on its surface.

On May 13 of that year, 1942, German submarines sank the Mexican tankers Potrero del Llano and Faja de Oro. A little later, Mexico joined the Allies and sent a wing of fighter planes into the war against Japan. The babble of voices I would normally hear on passing by the German school had quieted down somewhat. Would Mexico do what France had done and put all German-speaking men behind bars, irrespective of their political orientation? Even immigrants without a homeland (*apátridas*) like us? Merely the idea of it was absurd. In fact, we were not harassed. But the administration under Ávila Camacho seized 346 German businesses; it also sent all fascists who were suspected of engaging in anti-Mexican political activities to an internment camp near Perote in the state of Veracruz, especially owners of coffee plantations in the state of Chiapas. It is remarkable that this was done, even though the general population was pro-German and hostile to the Yankees. Furthermore, hundreds of German and Italian sailors were interned when they had the misfortune (or were lucky enough) to be surprised by the war in Mexican territorial waters. That peaceful corner of Veracruz filled up with Nazis, who celebrated Hitler's birthdays enthusiastically.

For all that, I believe that there has never been a more peaceful country in a state of war than Mexico.

Chapter 16

THE FIRST YEARS IN MEXICO

For three years we attended the vocational school of the Polytechnic Institute. Carpentry we learned from a teacher whom the students had nicknamed "Tin-Tan" because, like the famous Mexican comedian, he wore stretch pants and two-colored shoes. He made us smooth boards until our hands had blisters. We were taught metal crafts by "El Oso" (the Bear), who was exceedingly precise in the use of his square when he checked our welding. Once when I was working on a piece of metal, my hand slipped and the iron file pierced my thumb, leaving a scar to this day. In the class on plaster modeling, we were required to produce hundreds of angels' faces to be used as decorations in government buildings. In the foundry, I touched a length of iron that was still hot. In the plumber's shop we tried to make buckets which were given to the poor. Well, the very poor. And in an environment that smelled of burned rubber and constant short circuits, we were initiated into the secrets of electricity by Master "El Chispas" (the Spark). That was the time when we tried to learn a trade. In my case, it was a completely fruitless effort. I had, as the saying goes, two left hands.

In those days, we also had our troubles with math teachers. One of them, Pascual Rivera, kept calling my brother "Elmet." The other one was Enrique Zepeda, who let no opportunity go by, as he explained fractions and square roots, to imbue us with the spirit of Mexican greatness. The Spanish teacher, Catalina Herrera, tirelessly devoted to making us into "decent people," kept saying to our classmates: "Show them respect! Do not teach them rudeness!" She meant my brother and me. Once as I was entering a classroom, I picked up a piece of paper off the floor, which act Doña Cata praised by saying: "Decent people are orderly." At the end of this period, I found out what "*pamba*" means: getting bopped on the head by the whole class.

During our third year in school, Spanish was taught by Carlos Peña González, the president of the Academia de la Lengua Española en México. He was a teacher who, despite his high position, was there to make cultured people out of us. It was his habit to say: "What does the donkey know about saffron!" no doubt in order to encourage us to strive for the higher spheres of wisdom. It stays clearly in my mind that he made us read sections of the *Divine Comedy,* which I found rather boring, and excerpts from *Don Quixote,* which opened a completely new part of Spain to me, as well as works by Manuel Gutiérrez Nájera and Justo Sierra.

Our English teacher was Ema Cos del Prado. The skills we learned from her nourished our hope of using them on one of the American girls who participated in the summer courses. It was our greatest desire "to go out with" a gringa who was blonde, curvy, and the owner of a convertible. In the end, I managed to get hitched to one of these wondrous beings – without a convertible! Yes, in 1981 I married again, this time a North American woman, Joan Brodovsky, whose background is similar to mine. I still share my life with her as I am writing this. Thank you, Doña Ema.

Perhaps thanks to the strongly nationalistic inclination of a bureaucrat who didn't consider it important to be knowledgeable about what was going on beyond the borders of one's own country, our history classes concentrated almost exclusively on Mexico. The streets of the city were a different kind of instructor. Strolling through the center of town, I learned how to distinguish between heroes and non-heroes. Frequently we had to go to the Office of Immigration and Naturalization to get our permanent-residency permit. My story "El Guarura" describes its ambience. This office was at that time located on Calle Bucareli. I found out that this street was named after Antonio de María de Bucareli y Ursúa, the progressive viceroy of New Spain. Soon I noticed that there was no Hernán Cortés Square and also no Avenida de los Cristeros, even though Mexico is a thoroughly Catholic country. Since I found no Maximilian Street, I concluded that he must have been one of the bad guys. But I believe he wasn't quite so bad that he should be denied even a small square named after him. I learned why Santa

The Schwebels in Chapultepec Park,
Mexico City, about 1947

Anna was downgraded, lending his name to little more than a small alley; why Don Porfirio Díaz and Alfonso de la Huerta had been banished to outlying districts; why Isabella of Spain had been forgiven the Inquisition and why a street was named in her honor. And who may that San Juan de Letrán have been who had a whole avenue to himself? Also, Calle 16 de Septiembre would always remind me that I share my birthday with Mexico's Independence Day! And I? Would I ever amass so many accomplishments as to deserve one day being memorialized with a dark little street known as Callejón Don Bruno?

At that time, my brother and I entered into friendships that were to last a lifetime: with Luis Guerrero who often came to see us and most fondly remembers my mother's apple strudel and her Mardi Gras doughnuts; with Óscar Frank Leal, for many years Helmut's special pal. There was also Fortachón Macín who invited us once to Chalco where we stuffed ourselves on cheese from the dairy his family owned; "El Lagarto" (the Lizard); "El Barril" (the Vat) Carillo; "El Chato" (Snub Nose) Lavín; "Pinche Chilindrina" with his permanent acne – everybody called him by this nickname, and I thought for a long time that these were his real names. And there were many others whose names, however, have slipped my mind.

My best friend was Jorge Escartín. Part of the way to school we walked together, playing toreros with the passing cars, a skill that came in handy a dozen years later when I found myself confronted with a young steer during a tequila-happy company party. We also told one another dirty jokes (a first for me) and we practiced *rayuela* (flipping coins) and "heads or tails" so that I would not always lose against my namesake Bruno, who sold meringues at school. We all had nicknames. My brother, with a large nose and taller than I, was called "El Alcayata" (the wall hook); I, chubby and certainly no incarnation of the Mexican macho, was "Brunhilda"; and together we were "El Diez" (the Ten). Yes, I had visibly recovered from the hunger years in France.

Recently I was pulled over on the Anillo Periférico (the Loop) by a motorized traffic cop. After he had asked for my license in a gruff voice, he grinned: "I just wanted to say hello, Brunhilda, old pal. Don't you remember me? And your brother, El Alcayate – does his handkerchief still flutter that way when he is blowing his nose. Give him my best regards!" This was the guy who sat next to me in class. It's a mark of distinction in Mexico to have a nickname, and I have a great deal of respect for those creative linguists who have mastered the art of characterizing a person that way.

One of the most embarrassing experiences for me was the arrival of a health commission which was to examine the students for venereal diseases. We had to line up in the schoolyard and drop our pants and underwear. Our general attitude was: "Why the devil don't they examine their own whorish mothers?" There was no shortage of shy sidelong glances and nervous giggling, whereupon the physician on duty walked up and down the lines. I refused to be examined and started crying. Was that the circumcised Jew's panic? Recently Luis Guerrero reminded me in a conversation that Óscar Leal, another of my earliest friends, took me in his arms to console me. It was only in the safety of the sickroom that I showed what I had to show.

It was one of our most cherished pastimes to holler suggestive comments at the German girls on their daily walks to the Colegio Alexander von Humboldt and to secretly watch them during their outdoor gymnastics classes. Even today, a number of friends who attended this institution at that time and in years to come remember how bothersome it was for them to pass by our school. But they won't get me to feel guilty about it.

How would I ever forget the warm *bolillos*, filled with refried beans and hot sauce, that Doña Juanita prepared for us for ten centavos? Or the *tacos-de-chicharrón* vendor who approached our school shouting "Here comes Chicho-Mex?" But our favorite pursuit was going to the lake in Chapultepec Park and squirting water at the girls or watching three features at the flea-infested Cine Primavera for ten centavos. We also frequented a nearby billiards parlor from which the school prefect, Mr. Argudín, would sometimes evict us. Once, as a kind of revenge, all of us shouted together: "King Kong, Gunga Din (popular movies at the time) . . . the biggest bugger is Argudín!" Often we also hid from him in a wide, empty, unused safe, a remnant of the former shoe factory.

Years later Master Argudín and I were colleagues in a trade school. We both taught calculus. One day I brought this incident back to his mind and confessed my participation. He forgave me and we remained good colleagues.

But for all that, our Spanish teacher accomplished her purpose: most of her students became decent people. I have no doubts about that.

And for all the mischief we were up to, we did learn something. Even though my brother and I had joined a class in progress, we didn't have major problems during the first year. We got a ten in Spanish, the highest grade. English? A piece of cake. And while I had acquired one or the other scar in shop, I passed all subjects, the same as my brother.

By the end of summer 1942, Hitler seemed to be master over all of Europe. His U-boats controlled the Atlantic, and the Mediterranean, surrounded by countries under fascist rule, was in the hands of the Axis powers. The Sixth German Army had advanced all the way to the Volga; in August it stood before Stalingrad. The attack on the Russian defensive lines started on December 12. The Battle of Stalingrad ended at the beginning of February 1943, with a Soviet victory. In this dramatic confrontation, the German army suffered its first catastrophic defeat on its march of conquest, which caused great elation among us, perhaps for the first time since Hitler's assumption of power. I am convinced that Stalingrad, after which the Soviets increased their arms production, marked the beginning of the Third Reich's destruction.

On Saturdays the members of the group Alemania Libre had their meetings. They held long discussions about the political and military situation to keep up with the course of events in Europe. It is with full sympathy that I remember Klaus Bodek (died 2001) and his brother Uli, Ruth Stavenhagen (Klaus Bodek's wife) and her brother Rodolfo (a renowned anthropologist), Friedrich Katz (a first-rate historian and sociologist), Doris Katz, Alex Meisel (years later a famous cell biologist), and half a dozen others.

The leftist leaders of the group also organized meetings with famous writers like Egon Erwin Kisch, Anna Seghers, Bruno Frei, Lenka Reinerová, and Bodo Uhse. Kisch impressed me with his solid view of world politics and even more with his adventurous life, which he has summarized in part in *Marketplace of Sensations*. I especially have in mind a story about a village – in Belgium, I believe – which housed mental patients who were only a little crazy as boarders, and where families were held in suspicion if they could not provide room and board for these people. During this time I was also an avid reader of *The Seventh Cross* by Anna Seghers. But I had no great interest in the doctrinaire lectures. Today I wonder how much politics a boy of fourteen can digest when his heart is really set on watching a Tarzan movie or hiking up the Xitle the next day.

Some of my most beautiful experiences in the company of this group were the outings. I have fond recollections of a weekend in El Chico where, singing and goofing off, we made ourselves comfortable in a house that belonged to a couple of old maids. While climbing Las Monjas (the Nuns), a well-known rock formation, I got myself stuck in a spot where I couldn't move up or down until my brother and another friend helped me out with a rope.

Yet this dangerous incident did nothing to dampen my adventurous spirit. I started to idolize great explorers like Roald Amundsen. Later I added scientists like Darwin, Humboldt, and Schweitzer, and later Thor Heyerdahl. It was only during the 1970s that I became acquainted with the discoveries of John L. Stephens and his companion Frederick Catherwood in Mayan culture, to the point that I've always wanted to make a film about their adventures. What came closest to this dream was a project more than ten years later when I was still working for Televisa, Mexico's most important television network, and coordinated a high-definition video about the world of the Mayas. In order to take the spectator back from the present to the past, I moved the camera through the magnificent arch of the ruins at Labná and added an impressive trumpet-like sound made with conches as background music. I'll always remember this scene with a pleasant shiver.

On the suggestion of Luis Guerrero, I joined the Club Horizontes. We climbed the volcano Popocatépetl and the nearby mountain range called Ixtaccíhuatl and went on adventurous explorations of the underground rivers of Chontacuatlán and San Jerónimo, from which we emerged near Dos Bocas below the grottos of Cacahuamilpa together with swarms of bats, and had many other unforgettable experiences in a Mexico that was nearly unknown at that time.

I like to believe that twenty years later I passed some of this passion for nature and adventure on to my sons, René and Daniel. We spent memorable hours together along the Tolantogo, that turquoise-blue river gushing forth in cold and hot springs from a precipice, camping in the forests of Rancho Viejo, El Chico, and Los Azufres, swimming and watching the divers at the waterfalls of Agua Azul, and diving for ancient Mexican figurines in the Laguna de la Media Luna, which afterward we had to hand over to the military inspectors. No less fondly do I remember snorkeling among barracudas and manta rays and seeing boats that had sunk near the Isla Enmedio in Veracruz and near the reefs of Cozumel and Isla de Mujeres while sharks were watching us from below. Also the direct contact with the jungle and with the mangrove swamps in Los Tuxtlas, rafting down the Río Colorado, or the ascent to the ruins at the Cerro de Venado near Chimalacatlán (the topic of the following story) will forever live in my mind.

The German-speaking Jewish community united in the organization Menorah-Hatikwah. My parents didn't participate in its activities more than very occasionally, in contrast to my uncle Oskar, who was a contributor to the Tribuna Israelita, the Austrian *Arbeiter-Zeitung*, and other newspapers. My father avoided political discussions; he felt much more at home in an association called ARAM (Acción Republicana Austriaca de México) because it was not as strongly politicized as its German counterpart, Alemania Libre. For a number of years, this organization was headed by Rudolf Neuhaus, a dynamic Austrian, who was always willing to help to the best of his abilities. It was through this group that my father tried to get information about our relatives who had stayed behind in Austria. He never lost hope that he might find their names on the lists of refugees, but it was not until after the end of the war that his uncertainty was dispelled.

Chapter 17

Story

"YONKES" AND OTHER RUINS

He is wearing a wide sombrero made of plaited palm leaves and pulls cigarettes and matches from it, lighting a smoke at the flashing flame. In no time, the harsh and strong smell of cheap tobacco is spreading throughout my VW bus.

"As you can see, señor," the campesino says slowly, "we're having a pretty hard time here in Los Hornos. There's no future for the poor."

His name is Montes and he looks like Zapata. Come to think of it, many men around here look like him. Perhaps it's their eyes . . . their pride . . .

When I walked up to him in the village, the slow way he moved made me think that he must not be all there or that he was using his energy very frugally. I didn't notice any evidence that he was drunk. It was also quite possible, of course, that the expectation of being shaken out of his end-of-the-week boredom had sobered him up. A brooding heat had descended on the parched esplanade and on the cacti and *huisache* bushes lining it. The chickens were scratching the ground with their beaks open, the dogs refused to leave their shady places, and the flies circled a few piles of manure in slow motion. In the shade of a *framboyán* tree, we agreed that he would guide us to the ruins of Cerro del Venado, but there was no way he would let me broach the topic of money.

"We'll take care of that later, patrón . . . No problem . . . Let's not argue about that!"

While we were still on our way to Chimalacatlán, Chímala, as the people there call it, I observed our guide discreetly after he had rolled down the window so he could spit vigorously. His eyes were irritated, probably owing to their constant exposure to the dazzling sunlight. His hoarse voice, I'm sure, was the result of too much smoking and hard liquor. He is tall and lean, tough as leather, as they say. His black eyes gave a piercing look. Miserable teeth. And then this huge mustache with its gray-yellow corners that he keeps flattening with his index finger, in remembrance of the rebel from Anenecuilco. My imagination makes him wear Zapata's *jarano* and I'm silent, captivated by the impact of my visions.

"Have you noticed, Mister, the sad shape we're in over here? And you, from the other side, you're doing just fine, right?"

Sure. He thinks my sons and I are gringos, of course, but we are used to that. And when I look around, I have to admit that he is right. The land is cultivated only during the rainy season, the soil full of stones, paltry corn, the hills all around hard to farm, barren ravines.

"Yeah, where you come from, America, beautiful place. Just got back from there. I know what I'm talking about. Saw everything with my own eyes. All of it just very beautiful, honest to God. Just for the fun of it, me and three buddies from Jojutla went over there to try our luck. As braceros, is what they call it. But you know all that. Being that you *güeros* are from over there. Is a lot of you there. And the way everything is running smoothly! I truly admire that; my compliments! Honest to God, Mister! How good life is to you, no doubt about it."

The first thing I do, of course, is to explain that not all *güeros* come from "over there" and that there are some who were born in Austria, like me. And when his face lights up and he mentions kangaroos, I have an instantaneous vision of the Vienna Woods crowded with these hopping creatures.

"Let me tell you all about it. Just for the heck of it, I told my buddies that we should go to Tijuana and pick up a bundle of dollars. And then we took off, sí, señor. But let me tell you, up there, everything is quite different than we are used to here. Was a good experience, honest. We passed through a whole bunch of little towns. And then the ocean! Truly very beautiful, señor. Saw it from the bus. And then farther up north, nothing but barren mountains. If we down here are in a bad fix, then those up there are knee-deep in it. That's the honest truth."

I ask myself what this trip to the North must have been like. It probably was an unforgettable experience for these men. One can easily imagine that they tried to absorb all the details of this trip with their eyes and mouths open. I'm sure their "Look over there, paisano!" and "What do you say now, compadrito?" became more and more frequent, uttered with increasing enthusiasm. But soon enough they would have missed the smell of burned sugar cane and with it their wives and horses and the blooming jacaranda trees. They must have been amazed at the unendingly long drive through the Sonora desert and, farther north, at the miles of furrows running through plowed farmland and its muddy irrigation canals. The modern agricultural implements and the gigantic silos must have left an equally strong impression. They saw run-down little towns with bars that announced quite unabashedly "Nacho's Palace. Ladies Welcome." They went past little ranchos, saw the ever-present diesel barrels, the laundry flapping in the wind, their dogs, chickens, rusted roofs, and walls built from any type of material, crooked windows, old tires, and garbage. Somehow everything was so alike and yet so very different than what they knew back home. On their arrival in Tijuana, they would surely have wondered about the dusty mountain slopes – covered with wretched shacks – about the tourists, the all-night bars, and the *yonkes*.

"In one of these *yonkes*," Montes continued, "we spent our first night in Tijuana. We hadn't found a place to stay for the night and finally we ended up in one of these auto graveyards. 'You can bed down wherever you want but you use that corner back there when you need to piss and shit,' the owner had told us to our faces. I liked the way these people talked, straight to the point. Chema, that moron, only laughed like he was stupid because he couldn't find a car with enough upholstery for his long bones. I hunkered down in a Chevrolet, not bad at all. The things these people throw away as junk, truly a shame!"

I have seen it often enough myself on my trips to the border, the way the braceros come out in the morning when the fog lifts, carrying their bundles and their metal suitcases. They emerge from the *yonkes*, from the abandoned freight cars, from the decrepit hotels. Hunched-over figures trying to stomp away the coldness. They push each other for the fun of it, jostling for the sunny spots. And then they glumly get in line to take care of the formalities required on the Mexican side, braceros full of illusions and disappointments.

The rocks are cracking under the wheels of my minibus. We leave a thick cloud of dust behind us. Campesinos on their horses come our way and Montes greets them the way a general greets his troops, by slightly lifting his index finger. The trip to the North gave him a good deal of recognition.

"That was Dimas, a relative of Chucho, who I went across with. But the migra caught that idiot in no time. We had been hanging around the offices in Tijuana for quite a while without success. And if I had known how damn cold it gets up there and how few actually get a *permiso*, I wouldn't have been stupid and left my rancho. And then all the money I had left in my belt was just enough for one week of poor food. The thousand pesos I had taken with me had disappeared, and I told my buddies that this was it and we jumped the fence which isn't all that high anyway. I hid in a ditch first thing, but those two morons started running and the migra caught them right away. I met them again back here in the village when I returned and we laughed and laughed."

We drove on very slowly. The car creaked and bumped along a dry river bed which during the rainy season empties into the torrid Amacuzac.

"But they didn't catch me," Montes goes on, constantly hawking, spitting, and smoking. "I asked for a job all over the place but after a while I got tired of everybody acting stupid. There are people who are just as dark as the likes of us and they don't even answer you, believe me. So pretty soon I had it up to here and made it back to Tijuana. But you've got a real nice place over there, I got to give it to you. My respect, by God! . . . And those *frevais*, señor!"

We drove up a dirt road that truly was no freeway. Far, far away on the horizon we could see the bluish silhouette of the Sierra, its outline sharply defined by the transparency of the sky and seemingly quite close. We are coughing all the time due to the dust and the smoke in our car, and Montes burns his fingers on his cigarette, completely lost in his memories.

"Everything so clean and orderly. You have everything, honestly! And then one gets to this side, to Tijuana, and there's nothing but dirt and potholes. No comparison! That hurts a lot! One has to be honest about it! And to earn a little money for food, I washed cars and did all kinds of odd jobs. But competition is tough! There were many compatriots in the same situation."

I imagine these men returning with empty pockets, coming back to their village with a few American shirts and perhaps a small radio. Only now I notice that Montes's jacket does not look Mexican. That's probably why he doesn't take it off even in this heat! It's easy to imagine the jokes in the village, over drinks in the cantinas. But also the admiration for the adventurer and his stories of the money that had disappeared.

As soon as we arrived in Chímala, we started hiking up Cerro del Venado, slowly. On its summit, large, chiseled boulders awaited us, some of them weighing tons and forming the walls and terraces of an ancient Mexican pyramid. And questions came up like: "Who were they?" and "Why here of all places?" and above all "How?" since no stones of this size can be found for miles around. Even Montes scratches his head as he looks down the steep slopes once again. With an almost passionate pride, he points out various details in these ruins. Then we join him silently for a while, accompanied only by the gentle moaning of the wind and by the noises small animals make as they scurry across oak leaves. Sitting on a piece of history, we let our minds range through the wide sierra and are amazed at the minute size of the sheep below.

Stumbling along in a daze, we start our descent. We peel oranges we had brought along, all of us in a bantering mood. The noontime heat produces in me the feverish vision of a freeway bypassing Chímala below us, and another one of a *yonkes* covering the ruins. I consider it appropriate to tell Montes that two thousand years ago when this pyramid was being built, nothing existed as yet "over there."

And after a long time of silence, the campesino said to me pensively: "There's something to your idea . . . You know what? . . . I believe that we aren't in such a bad fix here after all . . . Or what do you think, patrón?"

Chapter 18

Story

THE GUARURA

"How do you spell 'Santa Rosa', one word or two?"

I am at the Immigration Office to have some corrections made in my documents. The waiting room is full of people and overflowing archives with well-thumbed bundles of files. And there is also a desk, no doubt from the time of the Revolution. Its condition as well as the scarred face and hands of the stout old man who mans it can tell you something about the course of the past sixty years, many of them marked by times of unrest and violence.

"So, how 'bout it, my friend? . . . One word or two?" the giant asks.

The Spaniard so addressed answers and then continues his quiet conversation with a compatriot. Deeply involved in his work, the old man goes on typing with one finger. He has to bend his massive back far down.

"'scuse me again, my friend. How do you spell '*llaves*'?"

"That's all right. Double-l and 'v'. You writing a letter?"

"No, not a letter. My boss, I mean the man who's going to be my superior, wants me to give him a written something . . . whatever it's called."

"Oh, probably a curriculum vitae."

"Yeah, yeah, exactly . . . They want to know what I've been up to. Just imagine, my friend! My whole messed-up life . . . Hardest thing I've ever done . . . I've been sitting around here since morning and can't get going. That's not fair, I tell you. I've never been a burrocrat . . . My work's always been outdoors . . . with weapons! . . . Give orders! And now I'm stuck here messing around with this idiot machine. It's not fair, I tell you."

All conversation stops. Some of the people in the room are shocked and are looking at the walls, embarrassed. Others are shaking their heads, and one of the Spaniards laughs out loud as if he had heard a good joke. But most of them show no reaction because they are foreigners and didn't catch what was happening. Now, amidst the silence, the old man's voice can be heard, loud and clear.

"How do you think I lost my fingers? Got them stuck in a desk drawer? Or from all that typing? No, my friend! Not me! That's why this nonsense here is an injustice. Just because I can't shoot any longer, they send me here . . ."

Waiting in a government office is an art all its own about which one can write a long treatise. If you don't have the situation under control, you are liable to get wrinkles prematurely and turn greensick. My most favorite technique for coping with this experience is to think up stories at the expense of others.

Let's call him "El Yaqui" and assume that he was, as the saying goes, strong as an ox. Well, he still looks like that. I would like to see him as the right hand of a rebel general from the Revolutionary Wars. So it's easy to imagine the Yaqui obeying Orozco's word, and all the others - soldiers' wives, cooks, mules, the troops, and the dogs – following the Yaqui's orders. Promptly and without hesitation – or else they'd risk life and limb. The game of power was the essence of his life. But more than power per se, he enjoyed putting it on display. That is what his voice, his .45, his posture, and not the least his gigantic hands let you know.

The Yaqui had grown up in one of the remote sawmills in the mountains of Chihuahua. At the age of ten, he was already chasing deer and practicing how to use weapons, and at thirteen, he could swing an axe as well as his sixteen-year-old brother, Lencho. A short time later he came down into the valley to join Orozco and his people. He had been with the troops for a few years when the Federales caught up with him after a long pursuit. He had hidden near the sawmills of his childhood but was betrayed and arrested.

He had by then spent six years in the jail of Santa Rosa de los Minerales when he heard that the *pelones* were approaching. He knew that he was a goner because they didn't waste any time and would shoot him on the spot. A few barefoot Tarahumara Indios who had been hired as outside guards were fighting the cold by stamping on the ground. He was the only one in his cell. Two women were squatting in the one next to his: a young one, ragged and high on marijuana, and on old one bearing her misery crouched in a corner. The jailer, a dark-skinned fellow of uncertain age and with a dense mustache, was using a *comal* to warm both his tortillas and his hands. He paid no attention to the girl's prattle, pulled his blanket tighter around his body, and started chewing.

"Do you spell Abelardo with a 'b' like 'burro', my friend?" the old man now asks the Spaniard and once more interrupts the mumbling in the waiting room.

"That's right," is the answer he gets.

An employee disappears behind the boss's door, holding a greasy little packet and a cola. Slowly the old man rises, rearranges his balls, and sits down again.

"Your brother'll be here in a minute with your food. What's his name again?" the jailer said.

"Abelardo."

"Waste of food. Tomorrow the bullets'll tear your guts open and send those good beans along with your shit to the devil!"

"Kiss my ass!"

It was the middle of January, with snow falling and a nip of frost in the air. The people of the village were tense as they waited for the column of government soldiers that was soon to arrive from Chihuahua. But even so, they all appeared to pursue their daily business calmly, as if nothing unusual were about to happen.

Abelardo slowly walked down the trail from the village to the jail, bringing what was perhaps his brother's last meal. He was crying as he stumbled along.

The jailer regretted having been so aggressive because a fellow like that Yaqui was nobody to fool around with. The two broads could have heard what he'd said. And this guy had a brother and friends who might take their vengeance.

"Hey, you women . . . you want a taco?"

But the one of them in the corner did not move an inch while the other one, glassy-eyed, rocked back and forth. (Exactly like that old woman there who seems to be German, the one by the side of the Spaniard.)

"Now come on, you Yaqui. Have a big ol' taco before your food gets here. I didn't really mean what I said a little while ago. It just slipped out. Come on, it's still warm," said the jailer as he approached the Yaqui.

Suddenly the taco so humbly offered flew through the air and slapped against the wall. A hand like a vise reached through the cell bars for the jailer's throat. The other hand undid the knot of the rope that he wore as a belt.

"Let's calm down! You know I've got nothing to lose. So it would be your bad luck to get yourself killed too. Now quit that kicking, old buddy, and let's be very calm. That's the way."

Without letting go of the jailer's throat he used his hand and teeth as he tied the rope into a loop and threw it around the jailer's neck, whose face had meanwhile turned the color of the dirty-gray cell walls.

"Take off your pants, and I mean now!"

"What are going to do with me? Come on, give me a break."

"You'll see . . ."

A forceful pull on the rope was enough to make the jailer obey. The Yaqui made sure that the pants would withstand a strong jerk before he tied them to the end of the rope which he kept firmly in his hand.

"And now, over toward the keys. Let's see how much more we need . . . And no tricky business . . . And not a word! If you try to get smart, I'll pull you back and you can figure out what'll happen next. Let me remind you I've got nothing to lose."

The jailer took a few hesitant steps and realized that it would take quite a bit more to reach the keys.

"And now back to me once more . . . And keep your hands low . . . Easy now . . . That's it."

The old man stops typing. He yawns while he unbuckles his belt. Is he going to the john?

The Yaqui pulled his pants off in order to tie them to the jailer's pants. That much added length should do it. But since he didn't want to risk losing more time, he looked for another piece of clothing. His shirt was too thin and a strong jerk would perhaps have torn it in two. But he was wearing a good pair of long flannel underpants that would do the job. A few quick maneuvers and the final extension was added.

"So, and now let's try again . . . But walk slowly and leave your hands hanging low. I warn you. You're a dead man if you try and reach for your rifle. The moment your hand makes a wrong move, I'll pull you here and I'll break your neck like a dry stick of wood. Hurry up, we don't have all day!"

As soon as his cell door was open, he could hear steps outside. Since he didn't have enough time to get the rifle, he jumped toward the door, knocking his brother down, and ran into the nearby forest. Abelardo picked up the pieces of food he had dropped, as if this were the most important thing to do but without losing sight of his escaping brother. The Tarahumaras, almost frozen stiff, reacted too slowly. When they finally got some shots off, his naked body was barely visible.

He went where no one knew him. After the Revolution he was assigned to be the bodyguard of an important politician, then was transferred to another one. And through all these years, he remained faithful to this occupation, the only one he really liked.

And then, my dear *guarura*, how is this going to continue?

Well, one day somebody decided: "The Yaqui? . . . What can you do with a fellow like him? Why don't you send him to the Immigration Office, to see Attorney what's his name? He's been trying for some time to hire someone to guard the entrance to his office, what with all those gringos and *gachupines* coming and going and no one to check on them."

And now he is sitting there, typing up the "something written" about himself, and his typing has become even slower.

"Listen, my friend! You know how to do this, don't you? What does one write at the end? . . . Most sincerely? . . . Your obedient servant? . . . Or what?"

Chapter 19

ACCLIMATING TO MEXICO

In contrast to the United States where anti-Communist policies proliferated without opposition, the left in Mexico was tolerated and experienced a strong boost under Vicente Lombardo Toledano and other leaders such as Fidel Velázquez. There existed at that time about twenty leftist groupings from different countries, all of them with a large number of Jewish members. The best known were Alemania Libre and the Heinrich-Heine-Club, which had originally been founded as a venue for cultural functions, but many of its members were constantly fighting with each other over political issues.

I've never had an opportunity to be a participant in world affairs, much less to influence them, with one exception forty years later. I played the accordion in a musical group which called itself Foreign Exchange. Our specialty was country and international schmaltz. Once we were asked by the U. S. Embassy to play at a reception in honor of the military attachés of the various diplomatic missions to Mexico. At the end of the evening, all of them were singing along with us, drinks in their hands, as East and West embraced and kissed.

The Heinrich-Heine-Club organized readings and theater performances. In a production of *A Midsummer-Night's Dream,* my brother excelled in the role of Puck. While he hopped around amid fauns and nymphs, I had to be content with moving props. That was my first contact with the theater, whose attraction was to hold me for the rest of my life.

Stimulated by the desire to have applause of my own, I accepted a role in *Snow White,* not to play a dwarf but the Prince. I also performed in a Jewish play at the Palacio de Bellas Artes, the opera house of Mexico City. But the opportunity to transform myself into a great actor did not arise until two years later when I was cast as the conceited barber in *A Little World Theater* by L. Gregory at the Teatro de los Electricistas, and as the young man who is in love with an older woman in James Matthew Barrie's *Rosalind*. The lady was Louise Rooner, the wife of the director, Charles Rooner (originally Ernst Robitschek), the perennial villain in Mexican movies. He always affected a slovenly look, with a moist cigarette dangling from his lower lip, and once during a rehearsal he asked me what I thought of his tongue which he presented to me, dripping with spittle, wagging it a short distance from my nose. Even though I had studied Stanislavski, I couldn't keep myself from blushing and stuttering in the love scenes with Louise, to which the audience reacted with laughter, one of the reasons I avoided the stage for the next twenty years.

I didn't return to the theater until 1972 when an English-language troupe invited me to accept a role in *The Night of January 16th* by Ayn Rand. This role was the beginning of my career as an actor and director, both as an amateur and later also professionally. My most memorable and cherished appearance was in Nikolai Gogol's *From the Diary of a Madman* during a week of performances at the Edinburgh Fringe Festival in 1981.

Since the allowance my father gave me was rather small, I started working during my vacations as an apprentice in an electrical shop in La Lagunilla. I wound coil for small engines and generators. After I tired of all that tangled mess of wires, I sold German thermometers to pharmacies. I was pretty successful, owing my success both to the "Made in Germany" on my merchandise and to my Austrian accent and Germanic appearance. I have no compunction about contributing to Germanophilia.

Early in 1943, I joined Club Deportivo Hacienda, a short ten minutes from where we lived. On Sundays I bought a bottle of Mundet soda pop and watched baseball games, trying to figure out their rules. Also, I played *frontón de mano*, a Spanish *pelota* game, which caused my right hand to swell and, at school on Monday, provoked taunts about too much "manual dexterity." At the pool I tried my first crawl strokes, perhaps intending to replace Johnny Weissmuller as Tarzan one day. I even practiced his famous shout, scaring whole flocks of birds from the peaceful Calle Tlaxcala.

My brother and I enrolled at the Escuela Artes del Libro on Calle del Oro in the Roma district. Every day we took one of the rattling buses that run up and down Avenida de los Insurgentes. Since stealing a ride is good for your coin purse, I learned how to play hide-and-seek with the conductors. But when they did catch me from outside through one of the windows or as I was trying to get lost among legs, I played the absent-minded gringo who had taken the wrong bus. The art school taught me block printing and woodcutting, lithography, etching, and other printing techniques. We also did nude drawing where, for the first time in my life and in great detail, I saw a completely naked woman. It is with great affection that I remember my teacher, José Chávez Morado, who was to become one of the best known Mexican artists. I went to see him in his studio in Guanajuato when, in 1999, I participated in the Festival Cervantes en Todas Partes.

On Sundays we drove out of the city to sketch, excursions that deepened my love of the Mexican countryside. Above all, I remember the aqueduct of Los Remedios a few miles north, the harsh region near Apan where agave plants to make *pulque* are cultivated, and the volcanic rocks of the Pedregal de San Ángel.

I started to feel at home in this environment and decided to study painting. One artist I greatly admired was José Guadalupe Posada, an engraver from the beginning of the twentieth century, whose works fill me with enthusiasm even today on account of their artistic expressiveness and political message. I was equally fascinated by the power of José Alfaro Siqueiros's paintings. One time we were taken to the Palacio Nacional to watch Diego Rivera at work. I was very impressed observing the Master in the act of making art, but even more I envied all those assistants swarming around him. Another painter who played a decisive part in my choice of a vocation was Joaquín Clausell, the Mexican impressionist. Together with other students, I visited the former studio of this extraordinary landscape painter in the attic of an old mansion which now houses the Museo de la Ciudad. I have never ceased admiring those paintings that the artist, already mentally deranged, created on the walls of his studio.

After three years of vocational school, my brother and I enrolled

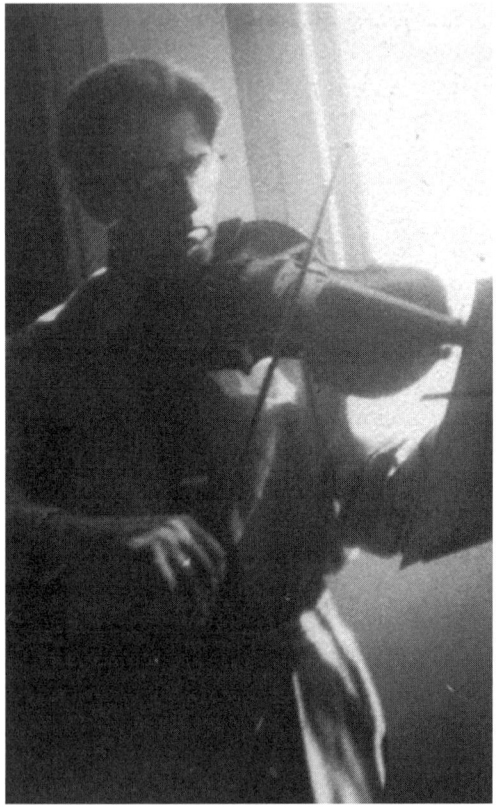
Father practicing, end of the 1940s, Mexico City

in an advanced class of the Polytechnic. We had to choose between engineering and architecture and both decided in favor of engineering. A little later, however, Helmut dropped out of school and started to look for work.

My father, speaking broken Spanish and Yiddish, continued to sell his gefillte fish, black bread, onion bread, challah, kosher wine, matzos, pickles, and other typically Jewish food. In order to help him out, my mother made farfel and mandelach (noodles to garnish soups). Above all, she baked cakes, something she would keep doing until the end of her life. Our store was located next to a filthy hole-in-the-wall that served hard liquor and was patronized by society's most depraved reprobates. Sometimes my father had to climb over drunks to open or, depending on the time of day, to close his security blinds. But for all that, he never ran into any trouble when at night he walked to the streetcar with the day's gross receipts in his briefcase.

I remember only one incident: on Saturdays I would help with home deliveries. One day I rang a door bell, holding a box of groceries. A very friendly woman opened. She took the box, said "one moment, please," closed the door and didn't come out again. Soon I found out that the apartment had been vacant for some time.

On some Sundays we went to Frau Bruder's restaurant on Plaza Ixtaccíhuatl to get the latest information about Austrian refugees and to eat goulash or other dishes Mama wouldn't normally prepare. After several months of hard work, my parents had earned enough money to take us to the Hotel Don Pepe in Cuernavaca for the weekend. The town at that time had a population of only forty thousand. On the main square was a coffee house which was operated by a compatriot of ours. There we enjoyed many a Viennese dessert, surrounded by laurel trees, *zanates* (a species of black thrush), and strolling guitarists. This was, unfortunately, one of the few vacation trips I took with my parents. Just as my brother and I did, they very soon went their separate ways.

After a few years, we moved to Calle Cadereyta in the Hipódromo-Condesa district, into a sunny apartment on the third floor, with many good-looking neighbors. Below us lived a family of Spanish refugees whose daughter, Meche Pascual, later became an actress. Lilian Welker, in the house across the street, had a career as a movie actress under the name of Lilia de Valle – I wonder what has become of her and her pretty sister, Marion. The apartment above the German girls belonged to a Jewish woman named Myriam and her mother. Miroslava, a very beautiful actress of Czech descent, lived across from us – tortured by depressions, she came to a tragic end. Below her, on the second floor, lived the Arispurus and below them the Ferraras with a daughter richly endowed with female charms and well protected by her strong brothers, César and Jorge.

Calle Cadereyta was a short street with little traffic, ideal for playing ball games. It is here that I had my first experience with American football which later turned out to be useful when I played in the lower division for the Polytechnic Institute. When we played soccer we tried everything to get a certain Mayoyo to be our goalie. The poor kid suffered from an illness that forced him to be in constant motion, making it difficult to kick the ball past him into the net.

At night we sometimes climbed onto the roof of our house to see if we might be able to witness something exciting behind the nearby windows. To give us a better view, we had to turn off the street lamp at the corner. It was my task to find the right cable, which gave me a chance to practice what I had learned from Master El Chispas. The admission fee for this pleasure was twenty centavos. These were good times. We even had a maid, a certain Hermelinda, who, when she was in a good mood, fixed four huevos rancheros for me and who was pursued at night by a good number of us. It is known that she ended up as a prostitute in La Lagunilla.

We also had a cat called Bussi, a name my mother gave to all her cats. On the advice of a so-called friend my mother bought *pellejos* (meat scraps) for our Bussi, mistakenly asking the butcher for a peso's worth of *pendejos* (morons), to the great delight of the other shoppers.

In order to overcome financial shortfalls, for example at five-o'clock-teas at the Loma Linda in the company of Alicia, during trysts with Lucrecia at the Aguascaliente pool, or on movie dates with Elisa, it was always possible to earn thirty pesos by donating blood at a blood bank. The only chance to get rich, however, was to visit *la cangreja*, a lottery vendor famous among the poor wretches and the central character in the story of the next chapter.

Lucrecia was a vivacious and vain art student who liked nothing better than to veil herself in captivating fragrances. One day I decided to hand myself over to the blood suckers so that I could buy her a good perfume, which made me feel like a wrung-out washcloth. Fortunately, Lucrecia lived nearby and on the ground floor. She opened the door and when she saw me standing there with my present in my hand, deadly pale and with wobbly knees, she roared with laughter, thinking this was one of my usual jokes. When she announced in a seductive tone of voice that she too had a present for me, I couldn't even summon the strength to blush.

On another occasion, I took a different girl friend, Elisa, to the movies to see *El Gran Vals*, a film about the life of Johann Strauß. It was completely beyond her why I simply couldn't stop sobbing when Miliza Korjus, walking in the Vienna Woods, sings "Viennese Blood." Another time I had the idea of using butter as a hair gel before going to a movie with her because I had run out of Vaseline. As soon as we had snuggled down in our seats a swarm of flies started buzzing around us, and my Elisa left the theater in a hurry. I watched the rest of the movie by myself, furiously sawing the air, which made the people next to me keep a suitable distance.

On the corner of Calle Tamaulipas and Calle Juan Escutia was a pharmacy where a somewhat older woman waited on customers, never missing an opportunity to flirt with me. One day she invited me to spend the weekend with her. My male pride made me say yes, and we agreed on a place to meet. Fortunately, she stood me up, and I was pretty relieved – even though I had missed a good chance to enter into a world about which the other boys were telling so many wondrous things. Henceforth, I bought my aspirin somewhere else and read the newspaper headlines at a different kiosk, far away from that pharmacy.

Ever since that decisive D-day, June 6, 1944, when the Allies landed on the Normandy coast, I had not missed an opportunity to follow their advance on French soil. I often went to the movies to watch the newsreels and all those American war flicks with Errol Flynn, who was suspected of being a secret Gestapo agent, and with Robert Mitchum, Burt Lancaster, or Ronald Reagan, all of them heroes whose inexhaustible vitality destroyed their enemies in a spectacular manner. I watched these movies over and over and over, nothing less than obsessed with these screen idols. In my American uniform, I shot down all Nazis, and thoroughly did away with them.

On May 6, 1945, the German troops surrendered at Reims and a few days later also in Berlin. The Allies had been victorious, the war in Europe was over. The crematoria stopped belching smoke.

As early as the middle of 1943, *El Libro Negro*, published by El Libro Libre, had pointed out the horrors committed by the Nazis. Had our relatives survived? Who of our large Jewish family had been able to save themselves? Some time later, we received the terrible news: my grandfather had been killed at Treblinka on September 23, 1942; Aunt Helene had been deported to Lagov-Opatov on March 12, l941; Aunt Pepi, Uncle Simon, and my cousin Erika had been murdered in the concentration camp of Sabac in Serbia; Aunt Rosi and her husband, Max, had been deported from France to Auschwitz; Uncle Schamu had died in Czechoslovakia. My cousin Reni was fortunate enough to escape to Israel, and Lizzi (Alice), the youngest of all my cousins, survived by hiding in France.

On the Hössinger side, my mother's younger brother, my dear uncle Hans, had been killed on the Russian front as a German soldier.

My father more and more often started playing his violin; whenever I hear a Mozart sonata, I inevitably see him with my mind's eye: wearing glasses, fully concentrated on his playing, and I see myself, conducting Beethoven's Ninth in front of the record player with greater enthusiasm than ever before. Mother would frequently play her favorite records by Richard Tauber and Joseph Schmidt and, less frequently, would sing all by herself. While she cooked or baked cakes, we would hear her singing tunes like "Vienna, Vienna, you alone shall always be the city of my dreams." I am sure she dreamed about seeing her sisters and other relatives again.

But very soon it was obvious to my father that returning to Austria was out of the question for him, and my mother confirmed this opinion. It was a topic that was almost beyond being brought up and about which our family never spoke openly. I myself considered returning. To return to grandfather's garden, to the meadows along the Danube, and the forests around Neulengbach? Most certainly. Did I perhaps try to run away from the necessity of integrating myself into my new environment, permanently and irrevocably? I believe that too was the case. But to go back alone? Without money and without a trade? Return to a country where I would have to live with people who had sympathized with the murderers of my family or with those who objected to the Jewish blood in my veins? No, that was most certainly out of the question.

Chapter 20

Story

THE EVOLUTION OF *LA CANGREJA*

Whoever goes to Chapultepec Park early in the morning is very likely to run into Doña Anacleta, better known as La Cangreja.

You may, after reading this, be interested in seeing her with your own eyes, but you will have to get up at the crack of dawn and walk over to the Don Quixote Fountain. Soon you'll hear a twangy but strong voice: "Today's lucky tickets."

Yes, Doña Anacleta sells lottery tickets – even if it's still pretty damn cold at six in the morning. She pursues her business energetically and with dogged determination as if her whole existence depended on the sale of every single ticket. Her shouts penetrate the quiet and the morning fog like a ship's horn.

Doña Anacleta may be around fifty – even though it might well be ten years more because her busy activity has given her robust health and a constitution of enviable vitality. She is small, tough, and has an extremely quick tongue. On top of that, she has a peculiar way of walking and constantly looks like she's pregnant, which does not prevent her, however, from keeping step with her customers. These, with hardly any exception, belong to the species of over-eager nature worshippers whose intent it is to suck in Mother Nature's oxygen with every fervent inhalation.

And that is why Anacleta owes her livelihood to the fanaticism of these early risers. There are, for example, the dancing pugilists who work imaginary opponents over with air punches. In the course of time La Cangreja not only has learned how to offer her goods by holding the tickets right in front of the boxers' eyes, at the same time announcing the number of tickets she hopes to sell them. No, she has also learned how to hand them the desired number of tickets and dodge their punches, give them their change, wish them good luck, and then keep on running. But that's not all. She does all this in front of those among her customers who are joggers and she does it with an incredible technique of running backward.

For Doña Anacleta moves backward as fast as forward. It has to be mentioned that this strange style of locomotion that she uses to earn her living can be considered an especially interesting instance exemplifying the theory of evolution – according to which only those survive who best adapt to the requirements of their natural habitat whereas the weaker life forms are eliminated. Anacleta has successfully defended her place against her feebler competitors who, one after the other, have given way to her.

One of her customers is a karate fighter who takes special pleasure in coming very close to touching her with his air kicks. But she delivers her goods with the greatest precision and with the cool-headedness of a Black Belt, without losing her cool at this bone cruncher's impressive screams.

Every Tuesday morning, a group of managers gets together, takes off their shoes and socks, and rolls the cuffs of their pants up in order to splash through puddles and mud. They are the most difficult customers, seeing that they not only bespatter her and call her a "useless bad-luck crab," but they accuse her on top of that of stepping on their toes. And what's even worse, they hardly ever buy a ticket.

And then there is this German with his Doberman. His pride offended because this woman can run backward as fast as he runs forward and hoping not to have his view obstructed any longer, he at last succumbs to abject resignation and buys the cheapest ticket. His stupid dog keeps thinking that La Cangreja is inviting him to play and in his euphoria jumps around the two of them, which earns him a kick and the insult "You moron of a mutt" – which is his little master's preferred name for his companion.

The poet in search of inspiration she entices with words like "How's the art of versification, dear colleague? . . . I've got your lucky number right here! . . . But let's continue our business in bed, cold as it is! . . . Ha-ha-ha!" The man so courted is pleased with

Anacleta's impudence, and he always makes a purchase.

The yogi standing on his head gets to see the tickets upside down, of course. How else? The fanatical "push-ups guy" needs to have the tickets shown in a synchronous up-and-down motion before he might consider buying one, whereas the man meditating has the expected last digits transmitted to him via telepathic forces. It is indeed true what they say: Life is hard. One has to show a good deal of imagination to make a decent living.

But just like Darwin's species, Anacleta's ancestors have adapted to the struggle for existence through genetic mutations that quite possibly extend over many generations. Perhaps her father, running backward, sold "the lucky ticket" to Don Porfirio Díaz, her grandfather to the Emperor Maximilian, and if we were to go further back in her family's history, we would probably find that one of La Cangreja's ancestors, facing him as she climbed down the pyramids backward, had offered the "sure winner" to the Emperor Moctezuma on his stroll through Chapultepec Forest. And exactly here, in the efficiency of evolution, lies the big danger. Perhaps it will come to this (in spinning out this controversial theory, according to which an organ grows where it is needed) that Nature has already supplied our crab woman with the necessary abdominal muscles, creating the appearance of a pregnancy. And does the vision of a future Cangreja not disturb you, of a woman with completely pivoting knee joints, with toes on her heels, eyes at the back of her head, and who knows how many pincers to wave her lottery tickets?

That's why it is extremely important to make her work easier so that these outrageous mutations are not given further support. If, therefore, you should, early in the morning, hear the shout "Today's lucky tickets!" in Chapultepec Park, then quickly try to find the crab woman and buy everything – and I mean everything – she wants to sell. But when you do that, you have to walk backward or else she will.

Such considerate behavior will surely be rewarded: A lottery ticket bought while you are running in reverse is dead certain to be a big winner!

Chapter 21

STUDENT YEARS

When the War was over in May of 1945, I enrolled in the Escuela Vocacional at the Instituto Politécnico. In order to get to school, I took an early-morning bus but I never got there on time, even so. My excuse was that the teachers were always late themselves.

The campus of the Instituto Politécnico was spacious, with about thirty buildings constituting its core and housing the diverse academic divisions. The dissecting room of the Medical School where the cadavers were kept had no air conditioning, and one could watch through the open windows as the future physicians were poking around inside the stiff, black corpses whose stench could be smelled as far away as inside nearby buildings. The hall and the macabre pranks the medical students played with body parts scared off many students who might have thought about taking anatomy. I secretly congratulated myself on not having enrolled in this discipline but instead opting for engineering, even though reading the book *The Living Brain* awakened a certain interest in neurology.

Our program of studies concentrated on the "exact sciences" of mathematics and physics. I'll always remember the physics teacher who did not allow us to use a slide rule in order to solve problems in arithmetic, including square and cubic roots. "Use your skulls, gentlemen, and at night keep your hands on top of your bedcovers," he used to say.

At that time, I couldn't imagine that I'd teach math in these same rooms ten years later. As a teacher, I was fairly popular. During tests I moved my chair on top of the desk and used binoculars to make sure that nobody was cheating, for which reason they called me "Herr General." The students in a different group always rose respectfully when I entered. They had covered my desk with a table cloth and had put a pack of my favorite cigarettes, matches, and an ash tray on it. To the students with the best grades I made presents of little scientific books, publications of the Fondo de Cultura Económica.

During the 1980s I toured with a play, *Stefanie. Duet for One,* a drama by Tom Kempinski, in which I played opposite the title character, portrayed by my close friend, Susana Alexander. Once there was a group of fifty-year-old men in the audience who let me know after the performance that they were not theater enthusiasts but had merely come to find out if I was as good an actor as I had been a teacher. They were part of that unforgettable group of former students. Something similar happened to me with the chairman of the town council in a village of Michoacán state. He said, when I asked him over the phone for advice on the best location for a television transmitter that, if I were that same engineer Schwebel who had been his math teacher, he would roll out a red carpet to welcome me. Well, modesty aside, I would have been pleased to have had a teacher like me.

Farther off, away from the stench of the anatomy theater, was the stadium. I was more than ready for sports. After it had become obvious that I wasn't good at blocking shots as a soccer goalie – my nickname was "the German Sieve" for good reasons – I joined the American Football team. We were given white T-shirts and every player had to attach his number to it. Mine was ninety. Because I had stitched it on somewhat clumsily, my nickname henceforth was "go." Our coach was a man whose attitude suggested that he had few friends. He was called "El Yaqui." When he saw the size of my shoes, he made me the kicker, and so I became "La Mula Gringa." During games we were supported by cheerleaders, some of whom live in my mind to this day: the full-bosomed "Chonchón," "La Pera" (the Pear), "La Sesenta Grados" (Sixty Degrees), whose behind rose at an impressive angle, and "La Fea" (the Ugly Duckling), who did her name full credit. Yes, without a nickname one was condemned to a shadowy existence. At one time, my parents tried heroically to find out what kind of a sportsman I was and came to watch a game. I saw they were sitting far away from the fans. They left the stadium before the game was over and confessed that they had never caught on to what it was all about.

This was the time when my father sold his store in La Lagunilla in order to acquire one on Calle Sonora, two blocks off Parque México. This move to a safer part of town was a relief to all of us. His regular customers were the Ashkenazim of the Hipódromo-Condesa district. My father was known for his courtesy and his sense of humor, the latter a trait I inherited from him to some extent. In 1992, the Mexican publisher Universo/Diana brought out a collection of some of my humorous short stories titled *La Gordis y otros relatos*.

My mother helped as always to add to our family income by preparing her by now famous Viennese pastries. On some Saturdays, I helped with home delivery and used this opportunity to replenish my supply of Lucky Strike cigarettes, an effective means of impressing the female world and probably a reason for male moochers to seek my company.

In those years, my brother had already ended his student life to become a tradesman. For a time, he took over a small lending library in a garage of Colonia Condesa. I helped him out whenever my studies left me time. His clientele, mostly German-speaking senior citizens from the neighborhood, was sparse, which gave me an opportunity to acquaint myself with the classics of world literature. Helmut changed jobs frequently and always had money. I remember the way he showed up in his distinctive jacket with shoulder pads, beige with blue checks. It didn't take long before he bought a car, used, of course, a 1936 Packard, gray, twelve-cylinder – Wow, one would say these days – with a high girl-per-mile rating – an expression popular at the time of beginning automobilization. He was always accompanied by his friend Arturo Weichsel.

Arturo's parents were German Jews who had come to Mexico during the 1930s and operated a dairy on a rancho in Tlalnepantla. Jewish farmers? Impossible in Germany but here they were able to work without restraints. Sometimes Arturo would invite me to dinner, one rich in potatoes and cabbage, with his hospitable family. Every now and then, I would ride horseback through this

With Susana Alexander in *Stefanie. Duet for One.* Foro Shakespeare, Mexico City, 1985

area which at that time was pasture land interspersed with large fields of clover. Today this region is covered with factories which add a remarkable amount of dirt to the metropolitan air.

In 1947, I started my studies at the Polytechnic Institute for Mechanical and Electrical Engineering. It was a time when electronics was still in its infancy and chiefly dealt with sound and radio transmissions. I decided on these subjects because they might promise an occupation later in an artistic environment. During the years after school when I was doing technical work for television, I did, in fact, spend more time than necessary in studios, joining the milieu of actors, musicians, singers, and poets. I was especially fascinated by the weekly broadcasts of operas by a company of puppeteers, Rosete Aranda, and also by Pita Amor, who, with a deep décolletage and a seductive personality, declaimed erotic poetry. About twenty years later, at one of the performances of the play *Stefanie*, Pita, by then mentally confused, sat in the first row and got up at the dramatic high points to shout, loudly and with enthusiasm, "Bravo!" to us actors and especially to her adored friend, Susana Alexander.

In 2000, my classmates and I celebrated our fiftieth reunion in our old school building. When I saw so many former students, I came to realize that fifty years is a very long time. But so long as we

Classmates at the Technical University, Mexico City, 1949

remembered our nicknames, the wisecracks, the same old jokes, and exchanged the usual questions like "Do you remember how..." and "I'm Pepe so-and-so, don't you know who I am?", these years seemed never to have gone by. We looked like bald-headed youngsters with wrinkles. Hugs were especially cordial since the erroneous rumor was circulating that I had died. The fact is, thanks to modern medicine and the knowledge and dedication of my wife, Joan, I had survived a rare form of cancer. This reunion was a good opportunity to talk about our lives.

I also had a chance to report on my long career in television during a time of dynamic technological progress, a good reason for bragging, I thought. Owing in part to my work at Televisa, this company has always been the technological leader among Latin American networks. I also wrote a textbook about testing procedures for television stations which was widely used by technicians. And I had to mention the project I consider the high point of my career: the construction of a kind of satellite that could transmit TV programs in high-definition format from the summit of a mountain, instead of, as is usually done, from space. The installation worked perfectly, but it was impossible to put it to commercial use. The originality of this invention aroused international interest, above all in Japan, a country to which I made frequent trips.

I talked about my two marriages, about my son René, his search for esoteric knowledge and his courageous determination never to

As the General in Jean Genet's play
The Balcony, Foro Shakespeare,
Mexico City, 1984

give up his fight against type 1-diabetes, about Daniel, my second son and his brilliant career as a graphic designer and as the artistic director of a television channel for cultural programs. And then there were the taunting comments of those who had seen me play a comic part in the movie *Ni de aquí, ni de allá* with the comedienne India María or in a theater as the General in Jean Genet's *The Balcony*: "For an engineer, you did a pretty convincing impersonation of that old moron."

My courses were not demanding, and I managed to get by with minimal effort, which meant I had enough time left for an occupation that had nothing to do with academic assignments: the game of chess.

There was a large billiard parlor on Calle de Allende, with a run-down room in back where a chess club known as El Tapanco had been set up. Its denizens played for money. One Friday I saw two players doggedly involved in their game. When I returned the following Monday, they were still sitting there, unwashed, sleepless, their eyes bloodshot. Their hands had left pressure marks on their glowing cheeks. The most obsessive one of the members was a Jew, a strong and aggressive player, who ran a store in this neighborhood. A sneaky fellow, he taught me the basic opening moves and a number of tricks from his repertoire. Soon he had gotten me to the point of playing for a stake, conceding me a few handicaps. Sometimes he let me win, but I often lost my whole allowance. Who knows why he called me "El Hombrovich," a nickname that stuck with me for a while among chess players.

A little later I started to play in tournaments, having joined the Club Metropolitano and the Ateneo Catalán, where I became friends with many Spanish Republicans. In time, I advanced to a higher category, and in 1959, I became champion of Mexico City, even though I lost against a young man who read comics between his moves. A year later, I played on the Mexico City team, and we became the national champions. I had the opportunity to challenge the later world champion, Bobby Fischer, and the Argentine Miguel Najdorf, at that time one of the world's best players. In each match I ended up with passable results.

Very much later, in the 1970s, I started to play "correspondence chess," which meant – in those days before the internet – writing a letter for every move. These matches often took years to finish. Once, in El Salvador, where I was installing a facility for videotape machines, I was eagerly looking forward to mail from one of my opponents, a Russian. His answer would determine the outcome of the game. At last a telegram arrived from my wife, Mati, in Mexico saying: "Soviet counter move . . .", followed by a series of four-digit groups of numbers such as are used in correspondence chess. As I read them, I realized that in those days of the Cold War I could be in trouble on account of this coded text. And sure enough, a short time later, I received an urgent communication from the Department of the Interior, calling me in for an explanation of a "certain telegram." I went, and over a lot of coffee, jokes, and shop talk, I

Chess champion of Mexico City, 1959

explained the whole thing to the official in charge who, as luck would have it, was a fellow chess player.

One of my favorite places to play five-minute speed games was, and still is, Cafetería Gandhi in Coyoacán. The many pretty coeds often made it hard to concentrate, as the story "Polish Opening" (Chapter 22) shows.

Whenever a professor skipped class, we would meet in a Chinese restaurant across from school or play billiards in a parlor around the corner. There was a rather crazy prostitute in this neighborhood, a poor woman who would grab our most intimate parts at the most unexpected moments. One day she was able to sneak into the pool hall unnoticed. To everybody's surprise, she appeared with her skirt pulled up at that end of the table where I was getting ready to make my shot. My cue left a hole in the table's felt.

Sometimes we would meet to drink beer in a cantina on Calle de Allende, owned by a Republican from Catalonia. We did drink but hardly ever to excess. Once, however, after our finals we decided to have a big bash. It was impossible to take the stein away from my friend El Sapo (the Toad) once he had hoisted it. At the end of our "session," he asked us to take him home, which we did – but without leaving the cantina. We shook him around for a while, at the same time imitating traffic noises, and finally he fell into my arms, repeatedly saying: "Sorry for that, mom . . . but I passed all my exams!"

When we were about to run short of money, we started to curse General Franco in exalted voices. "On the house!" our Catalan host would say and drew near to share in our conversation. This good man also permitted us to bring food into his bar. When it was my turn once to buy the snacks from a taco vendor on Avenida San Juan de Letrán, I ordered sixty tacos, whereupon this man looked me over from top to toe and asked me in all seriousness: "For here or to take home, young man?"

During my last years in college, I became close friends with Alejandro Bonilla. He often invited me to spend Sundays with his family. We played cards, chess, or ping pong. One or another of the admirers of his sisters was always present too. I was thought to be one of them since a few times I had dated the oldest girl, Beatríz.

One of Alejandro's uncles was the owner of a rancho in Tlapacoyan, a village between Tezuitlán and Martínez de la Torre in the State of Veracruz. He invited me to spend a few days during break in one of my last years at college. We were given a room with two beds, one of them occupied by a very long snake. The uncle said: "Don't be afraid," and shook the mattress, and the animal, called a *ratonera* (mouse catcher) in that part of the country, slowly wound its way off the bed and out through he door. It lived in the house and took care of reducing the number of rats and other vermin that its taste buds favored. I don't know how the chickens survived. There is no need to mention the absence of cats on that rancho.

The property extended for a few miles up to a wild raging river. High rocks afforded a panoramic view across a countryside of gentle hills, covered with banana plantations and meadows on which cattle, surrounded by herons, were grazing. In the distance, a river disappeared between ravines. Once we went hunting with small-bore rifles. We shot here, we shot there, but without success. That evening the owner of a neighboring rancho showed up, complaining that we had injured one of his cows. Fortunately, the man was a friend of our host. We apologized for our clumsiness, and the rancher laughed as he admitted that his cow may not ever have been aware of the hole in its tail. The whole thing was put to rest in the course of a boozy evening.

Another time, as we were having supper, one of the hired hands came into the dining room, pale as a whitewashed wall. He stuttered when he said that the "old woman" was in the barn. "It's an apparition that does her mischief hereabouts," said the embarrassed rancher. We got lanterns and went to the barn. There was an old woman, famished and dirty, cowering in a corner and trying to hide behind the implements. Asked where she came from, she replied "Santa Monica," whereupon the workers crossed themselves repeatedly. The next morning she had disappeared. I was told later that Santa Monica was the name of the village cemetery.

This incident impressed me so strongly that I wrote a story about it, "The Old Woman." It was the beginning of my career as a writer. But my serious involvement in this line of work didn't come about until the 1960s when I started traveling in Mexico as part of my assignments for television. My wife, Mati, and I were members of a group called Tirapiedras. On evenings full of music and literature, a book by the same name and with my first ten printed texts came into being; three years later the collection *Estimado Yo* followed, brought out by Diana Publishers.

Toward the end of our college education, we were sent to Gutiérrez Zamora, a village in Veracruz, for topographical studies. The arrival of a group of students from the capital city was an extraordinary event for the townspeople. Our job was to draw up a design to level the village street and the access road to Tecolutla. We were put up in an old house with a garden full of orange trees, with many rooms and as many types of vermin. Before calling it a day, we had to make sure there were no bed partners such as millipedes, roaches, lizards, or scorpions hiding between the sheets.

We were the center of attention wherever we went and people knew everything about us: that a surveying instrument had been lost, that one of us was suffering badly from diarrhea because he had eaten spoiled crabs, or that I woke up in the morning splattered with bird shit because I just had to spend the night in a hammock under orange trees. Another student became something of a local celebrity because he had to have an infected tick bite on his rear end treated at the hospital. Despite the jealousy of the male population, the girls kept inviting us to parties, which was not without its dangers if one didn't behave oneself. So we did our best, or tried at least.

At one of these evenings I met Michaela, the daughter of a wealthy family of French descent. While we were dancing she discreetly fought off my attempts to get closer, even though her thighs touched me and her glances invited me not to stop. The most daring thing I had the courage to do was to stroke her arm when her father was a little negligent in his chaperoning duties. Her skin was of a softness one can fully appreciate only in an ambience suffused with the fragrance of vanilla under a sky resplendent with all its stars and surrounded by the music of a marimba playing "La Rondalla" – En una noche clara de inquietos luceros.

After that evening we met two or three times, exchanging sighs and yearning glances. I invited her to come to Tecolutla for a day, which she firmly declined as if to say that decent girls could not drive to the shore with an unknown *güero* who hadn't learned as a child to keep his hands under control. She confessed, furthermore, that she had never been to the beach, a distance of less than eight miles, because the priest wouldn't approve of it.

One night all of us were at a party and I returned a little earlier than the others. I knew that my colleagues would be slightly befogged. Carefully I made drawings of scorpions on the walls near the beds and lay down to await the arrival of my roommates. What a funny thing it was to watch them in the semi-darkness, hopping on one leg and, with a shoe in hand, trying to kill the poisonous beasties.

At the edge of town, about fifty yards from the road to Teclutla, stood an abandoned two-story house known as "The House of Don Maximino." People in the cantinas said that the place was haunted and full of snakes and that we, if we were real men, would have to spend a night there. This business became a matter of honor with us. We decided to use the weekend when the night watchman was on a binge.

We took sleeping mats, flashlights, machetes, and a bottle of rum, and made ourselves at home on the second floor, assuming that snakes don't like to climb stairs. During the night there was no shortage of the time-worn pranks: moaning and tugging at strings that had been secretly attached to the sleeping mats. We did indeed behave like little boys. In the early light, we saw a snake rolled up in a corner of the room and another one between the metal bars of the balcony, even though they may just as well have been forgotten jute ropes. We didn't take the time to find out. When we returned to the village, our popularity increased considerably. This little adventure was a favorite topic of conversation for the rest of our lives.

Later, after I had returned to the city, I exchanged a few letters with Michaela and here confess that I had given some thought to keeping up this relationship in order to become, perhaps, the first Austrian vanilla planter in Veracruz. About twenty years later, this brief encounter with Michaela became the inspiration for a story titled "The Other Michaela," which has been published in the collection of short stories by the same name.

Even though in years to come I traveled a good deal in the State of Veracruz, I did not return to Gutiérrez Zamora until forty years later. I was surprised at the economic growth of the village. Perhaps in part due to the work of a few students from the capital? Why not! I circled the main square a number of times in my car and tried to imagine what would have become of me if I had married Michaela back then, that I would not be much different than the old men who enjoy the fresh air sitting on the benches of the park pavilion. For a brief moment, I saw myself lighting a cigar, straightening my typical Veracruzan hat, and contributing to the conversation in the accents of these coastal people, probably discussing the problems caused by artificial vanilla, and the goals the team from Pachuca had scored against Veracruz. And Michaela? Did she keep her graceful loveliness like some of the señoras promenading under the jacaranda and tabachín trees on the square? Even though it was afternoon and modern music was blaring from the loudspeakers of the pavilion, the tune in my head was "En una noche clara de inquietos luceros . . ."

Chapter 22

Story

POLISH OPENING

She was sitting at a nearby table sipping juice in small slurps, its carroty color reflected on her nose. And while my lips were blowing on a cappuccino to cool it, hers played an erotic up-and-down with the drink in her straw. I couldn't stop watching her: her pallor, the aristocratic profile, which contrasted sharply with the coarse, flower-embroidered *huipil* she was wearing, the straight black hair, the long lashes, and the eyes of a color that Sachertorte takes on when you are on a diet.

It was a lazy afternoon on an ordinary weekday. I had decided to allow myself a few hours away from work to play chess at the Cafetería Gandhi. As always, pop tunes coming from the radio, the music preferred by the personnel, disturbed an atmosphere tinged with intellectualism. The other guests didn't seem to mind, though, and some of them even warbled along with the crooners. But I was yearning for Chopin. Suddenly I felt the desire to have my elegant Polish opening accompanied by Chopin.

I noticed that her fingers were moving to a rhythm that clearly had nothing to do with the *cumbia* the radio was playing. Even though it isn't easy to concentrate on music while you are playing chess, I suddenly realized that Chopin had sneaked into the Caribbean rhythm. Yes, exactly, that certainly was a Prélude I associated with something extraordinary from the very beginning. It dawned on me that the music did not come from the record store below, but from where she was sitting. Did she perhaps have a cassette player with her? I observed her body at the start of a Rondo, as it gently swayed to the beat of a new rhythm. The same thing happened during the following Ballade. She looked at me in a very mysterious way.

This had happened only a few moves ago. How fast time flies during a game of chess.

She was very young, petite, and her body showed a gentle suggestion of curves. In harmony with the music, her skin began to reflect quite intricately glistening colorations that made my cappuccino turn into a dance of undulating flickers. My free index finger slid across still virginal thighs, warmed by strange musical networks of circulation. Was her sex perhaps surrounded by frizzy eighth notes? She behaved like someone who has found her vocation. She didn't say a word, nothing but Chopin was streaming out of her. Which instrument? No matter, which. Every one of them. She was a woman made of music.

The more the juicy yellow in her glass ebbed away, the paler her skin became. I observed that her glance, with no diminution of her yearning, searched out mine ever more frequently, casting a spell on me in a promising way. At the end of the Impromptu, she rose and left the cafeteria. I followed her. She moved with the elegance of a Mazurka. I noticed that she was looking at no one: I was the one she had chosen. I followed the musical breeze but kept a bit of a distance and thought that there was nothing unusual about it and that the Chopin emerging from it, just like the delight dahlias take in color, was the result of a development. I continued playing with my fantasies according to which women made of music exclaim arpeggios when they are born and when they die. This idea occupied me until the next intersection.

When she turned off into a narrow street, her rhythm segued into a Polonaise. Her flowing skirt made me think of sails bulging in the winds of Mallorca and her gait conjured images before my eyes of splendid concert halls with grand pianos, silk fabrics, and brocade. I heard the chords of a sonata. She stopped at a corner, where I caught up with her. The intensity of the sonata increased. I said "Te quiero" to her. She looked at me without revealing the emotions I had expected and we kept walking, side by side. She said nothing, not even that her name was Frédérique.

We kept walking this way for a while, silently, hand in hand, and I knew that I would find out later that we were marking out a gigantic clef. When dusk was beginning to fall, we reached Obregón Park. She undressed, sounding the Nocturne No. 12 (in G major, opus 37). She was trembling as she lay down in the bed of dahlias.

Back by the pavilion, a park guard was pumping up his bicycle tires.

When I lay down with her and touched her, she half opened her eyes and sounded a beautiful C-minor while her body produced strange harp-like vibrations. Even though at times she was visible only as a blur and was veiled in musical undulations, I sensed her presence to be excitingly real. As if in slow motion, I registered the trembling of her eye lashes, lids, and nostrils and felt the motion of her nipples as it made her small bosom heave with the deep sounds of this waltz. When I put my ear on her breast I could hear her heart in 3/4 time. I let my fingers slide all across her body and could feel the tiny hairs in her pores tingle. There was no way of telling where this music was coming from: her whole being was music. She exuded a musical waft of delicate filigree. When I kissed her vibrations, her body writhed with desire.

The park guard's pump was still squealing.

She spoke not a word. But the moment arrived even so when she half opened her eyes making her body quiver with the beautiful arpeggio of a gentle orgasm and exuding purple hues.

Then she looked at me as if I were an abstract painting, lowered her eye-lids and, after taking a final noisy slurp from her straw, asked for the check, warbling a mambo.

And my king was checked . . . almost checkmate.

Chapter 23

Story

THE OTHER MICHAELA

Ever since the Frenchman, riddled with bullets, met his death, Michaela's eyes have pierced beyond everything. She smiles, to be sure, but her smile is meant for the space between people. She speaks with the walls, with the corners, with the chalk board. With heavy breathing and an absorbent glance, she fondles the emptiness.

The children giggle and whisper whenever the other one appears, this other one who wipes away the beloved Frenchman of Miss Michaela, the teacher. They have come to be familiar with this other one, she with the face of a dead person. It always looks so funny when she follows Miss Michaela around, fluttering about her, constantly pulling down the hem of her skirt after having pressed her knees together or closed her décolletage and while she does this, incessantly fingering the crucifix resting on her own bosom.

"You must extinguish him forever from your life, Michaela. You'll know how," the priest had commanded her, enjoining her to pray a large number of Our Fathers. And with a deep sigh, the other one went to work to expel the Frenchman from Michaela's memory.

The Frenchman had come from far away. From very far away. From a country one sees in movies. From cities, from streets that exist only in movies. To put it precisely, from a world one could admire on a Sunday afternoon or Wednesday evening in Papantla if Mama was in a good mood. He had come with his smile, his cologne, and his talent for persuasion, with this strange way he had of pronouncing words. And those hands! He had come to create who knows what. Even for the other Michaela, it was more exciting to listen to the Frenchman talk than to go to the movies. He himself was the show, in color. He had brought the world with him.

"Be on your guard with this *güero*," her mother had said, this woman who, untouched by passion, had never sinned.

Michaela had never been to the beach, even though it was very close by if one took the new road, because it was something the priest didn't approve of. Also Rafa, her fiancé, had forbidden her to go. And her mother had told her that lecherous men would lie in wait for her there wherever she walked, and would try to steal her honor. She had told her stories of dangerous shadows along the country road and made the beach bristle with snakes. That's why Michaela had never left the village before. The other one would not allow it.

But in defiance of all this, she did, one afternoon when the sultry air, suffused with the scent of vanilla, was oppressively hanging over the village, go to the beach with the Frenchman. They took his motorcycle. Her dress and the other one fluttered around her like turtledoves. And as she lay in the sand, that one was unable to stop the waves that were rising inside Michaela. She couldn't prevent Michaela from getting to know life.

When they returned, death was not to be held back: Rafa.

For a week the Frenchman, lying under a blood-spattered sheet in the storage room of the municipal building, had to tolerate the jokes about how badly he stank. And when at last, his body completely bloated, he smiled, somebody from the capital came to take him away.

Rafa, who hadn't even been allowed to stroke her hair, hid out in Don Maximino's abandoned house. People told each other stories in the cantinas about how he had no longer been able to take all these snakes and had just run away. He took to his heels, but it's also possible that he had stayed somewhere closer by. Who knows.

"You have to erase the Frenchman, my daughter. Pray and forget him!" the priest had mumbled. His cassock darkened his face. Her aunts and her mother had given her the same piece of advice. Even the principal had told her that she shouldn't bring him to school with her any longer. What a disgrace!

From that time on, one can see the two Michaelas scurrying about the village, to mass at eight, then to the baker's, to school, to confession. The one completely distracted and the other one gesticulating through the air with a large, especially soft eraser (for especially cherished lines). She is always on her guard, this other one. As soon as Michaela's glance becomes lost in the distance, she hectically erases the Frenchman's silhouette and blows the crumbs away. In the classroom, she uses the chalkboard sponge and then fans even the last bit of dust away, while Michaela looks in the other direction with a sigh.

The two of them are inseparable. Together they circle the village pavilion against the flow of faces, the one whistling and gesticulating to herself, the other searching, incessantly searching between fragments of glances. One can also see them often by the walkway where the boats arrive, the one smiling or weeping, the other trying to smooth out her mouth.

Even at night they don't part company. Of course not, because the priest is on his guard. The other one is commissioned to see to it that Michaela sleeps deeply. And with mysterious maneuvers, she suppresses all things that may be able to emerge as a dream. Sometimes Michaela begs her not to extinguish her Frenchman without leaving a trace. Why couldn't she close her eyes just a little and merely blur his image? But the other one will not relent. She is not permitted to. She knows what she has to do.

"We must expunge him from your life, my daughter. It is a sin to continue fingering him in front of all these people, the way you keep doing," the priest warns her over and over again, drawing lascivious lines into the air with his index finger.

But even though they leave her not more than a few specks of her Frenchman's figure, Michaela goes on recognizing his lips in other people's lips, in everything red (he had had very red lips, the Frenchman). Then the other one transforms everything into a world without the color red: gray tongues, greenish skin; the stripes on the lighthouse turn black, true black.

That afternoon full of scents! She will not experience it again! The air is now pushed through a fine sieve, and the fragrance of vanilla disappears inexplicably. Even the stench of crude oil seems to have dissipated.

His hands! When the girl trembles because she sees his hands in those of the village people around her, the other one mutilates them. It seems quite weird to Michaela how one can cross oneself without fingers and write with the stump of an arm. She is very clever, the other one.

Yes, very clever indeed. Because when she sees that the hot wind from the south reminds the sinful girl of the Frenchman's breath, she stops the palm trees from swaying back and forth and ends the undulations of the tall grass.

His voice! She must not remember his voice! . . . And so only silent people walk around in the village, forcing Michaela, surrounded by silence, to communicate with this silence only through gestures.

"Extinguish him, my daughter! You have to extinguish this fellow again and again . . . Are you coming close to forgetting him?"

No, she does not forget. She stops in front of the candles, totally absorbed, whereupon the other one makes all things phallic disappear.

But then Michaela smiles at the force of the river in which she sees the tempestuousness of her lover. And even though the other one robs the current of its power, the Frenchman insists on his continued presence. Under the warm embrace of the shower (how tenacious this *güero* is!), she feels the tips of his fingers once more. When the other one turns the faucet to cold, Michaela imagines cool waves flowing around her body. When the ocean is erased from her touch, she smiles through the clouds, for the sky's blueness reveals his eyes to her. Whereupon the other one, sighing with great energy, makes all blue tints vanish. All of them. From the river all the way up to where the buzzards circle endlessly, there remains nothing but deep, colorless space. Spectral silhouettes are all the two of them are left with.

Then the other one usurps Michaela's smile and gives her in return nothing but her own deathly countenance. And quite gradually she first made the color red appear from out of the mass of nothingness. Lips, then hands, voices, music. Then fragrance of vanilla. Warmth and the color blue. Motion. Water flows again.

Then all things vertical. The masts of the crab boats return to their up-and-down. The columns of the church once more thrust upward. People walk again with their heads held high.

And then, very cautiously and with the grimace of an unaccustomed smile, the other one makes Michaela's Frenchman appear for herself.

Chapter 24

Story

THE OLD WOMAN

Wheezing like the old fuel pump, Satanas starts into his howls. And then he draws them out, with the neighborhood dogs responding as echoes from many directions. This appears to be the signal for the sun to extinguish its blazes and to vanish in a hurry behind the quickly darkening hills. The sultry air is oppressive, numbing. On the rancho that is nestled against the mountains, the frayed silhouettes of the banana trees stretch their stalks. All things are waiting for the coolness of night. A slight tremor, longing for a breeze with rain, runs through the leaves. In the distance, the reddish lights of the village are turned on, one after the other.

On the terrace the rope holding Don Fulgencio's hammock is squealing rhythmically under his weight. He's the owner. All around the rustle of invisible insects, the shrill evening concert of the cicadas has commenced. The voices of the hired hands returning from their baths in the creek a few hundred steps from the main house can be heard emerging out of the twilight.

Don Fulgencio perceives the arrival of his workers through the smoke from his cigar. He enjoys this hour before supper, alone with his thoughts and swathed in clouds of smoke that keep the mosquitoes away, fumes from the strong, locally raised tobacco.

"Evening, boss."

"Evening, *muchachos*. How was your bath?"

"The other *nauyaca* is still hanging around there, looking for the male we killed."

"Let's see if we can catch her tomorrow," Juan says, a tough old bird with gaps in his teeth.

"We'll see . . . "

"We saw her near the large *guarumbo* tree. She's one of the yellow ones."

"'We', that's plural," Isidro replied. "*I* didn't see a thing."

Juan is furious. His face is turning dark while he mumbles: "Damn Isidro. Always has to make trouble. You just wait till you run into me some day when I'm drunk or in a bad mood. He's just bragging because he went to school at the port."

And with a challenging flicker in his eyes, he adds that he is certainly not so stupid that he can't recognize a damn *sorda*.

But Isidro doesn't react. He turns round slowly and goes into the house. Don Fulgencio stops swinging back and forth and with a moan works himself free of the hammock in order to follow his men into the dimly lit room.

The boss always has supper with his *muchachos*. Nobody speaks. Isidro dips his bread into his milk coffee, looking at Juan from the corners of his eyes. Juan in turn stares at his plate, asks for the chili sauce without looking up, pours it over his beans, and starts spooning them up with a slice of tortilla. The buzzing of a mosquito increases the tension.

"The old woman is haunting the place," Juan says very slowly.

"What old woman?" Isidro's spoon drops into the glass with his white coffee.

"Don't play dumb. You know exactly."

"I've no idea what old woman you're talking about."

"You heard Don Ceferino say the old woman is haunting the place. And you heard her last night behind the barn. Don't act stupid."

"Isn't true."

"You're dumb, and deaf to boot."

Isidro tries to break the argument off and says emphatically: "I didn't hear a thing. And besides, things like that don't exist."

And with that he leaves Juan to his beans and to his grumbling out of which one can clearly hear "*cabrón sabihondo*."

"Juan," the boss says in a calming voice, "go and see to it that the animals are fed."

The old man rises, making more noise than is necessary. He wipes his beard, giving a loud belch, and disappears mumbling to himself. The others continue eating.

All of a sudden Satanas starts howling again. Then another dog. And soon thereafter a few more.

"Those curs have run off," says Chucho, the third worker.

But they are not barking after a bitch in heat. Their howling sounds like coyotes. But not quite. It sounds more like a wail, a soft, penetrating whimpering.

Something is going on. Nobody knows what, but the men stop chewing. Aware of a complete silence, they look at each other and feel a cold shudder running down their spines. The shrilling of the cicadas has died down; the dogs have stopped barking; even the mosquitoes no longer seem to be buzzing.

The men rise slowly, exchange tense glances, and go to the door where Juan runs into them. His face is a grayish white, like the whitewashed walls of the room, and his eyes are wide open as if they were about to pop out of their sockets.

"The old woman! . . . In the barn!"

"You're nuts," says Don Fulgencio. Yet they all are pushing to get outside.

"The gun! Quick, boss!"

The door to the barn is open. The animals are bunched up in a corner. Nobody is brave enough to step inside.

"Get a lamp!" Juan says to the others.

Shortly thereafter, Don Fulgencio joins them, his face shiny with sweat and excitement, holding his .38 in his fist, Isidro behind him with the light.

"What'd you see?" the boss whispers.

"She's back there . . . in the corner," Juan says.

"Who's there?"

Nothing. Only the unrest of the animals.

"You're drunk. Imagining things."

"I swear, boss. How can I be drunk after one sip! She's there. Gave me quite a scare."

"Somebody there?" Don Fulgencio shouts, cocking his weapon.

Nothing.

"This Don Cefe is just talking to sound important, and this moron here is drunk. There are no apparitions," Isidro mumbles.

At last the boss decides to step inside, his gun in one hand, the lamp held high in the other.

There, in a corner, the old woman is cowering. Living misery. Covered with pustules. A crooked grimace disfigures her black wrinkled face, like burned paper. Shiny spittle dribbles from her toothless mouth. An arm, skinny like a little dry twig, stretches out toward the group numbed with fear. It takes quite a while before the boss is able to say a few words.

"Who are you?"

The old woman doesn't answer. Only her fingers with their long filthy nails are trembling. And Don Fulgencio's legs buckle when he sees that she is as transparent as a specter, and he sees that Juan's hair is on edge, also Chucho's . . .

From the hole that had been her mouth she spewed a pestilential breath toward us that turned us into stone, so that we were incapable of moving, and then she opened her eyes wide, with sparks flying out of them, and her whole face looked like a black, rotting, worm-eaten pumpkin!

"Say something!"

She retreats farther into the corner.

"Who are you, I asked!" Juan says in a voice that is meant to sound firm.

Nothing. Only a fleeting, moist flicker from her deep eye sockets. A frightened look, pleading. The old man is terrorstruck when he sees, and he will see this for the rest of his life that she is beginning to hover, and he will tell in the village over and over again: – And her stench struck us like the stink from a putrid corpse, and her hands looked like the talons of a buzzard, with blood dripping from them, and I saw all this exactly the way I tell it because I swear by the Holy Virgin that I was not drunk . . .

But all she wants is rest from her misery. Peace. God's acre.

"Where do you come from, woman . . . or whatever you are?" Isidro makes himself ask, making the sign of the cross. The others do as he does.

But the woman shows no reaction. Only her emaciated body moves. The stench becomes unbearable. At last a slight trembling of her chin signals an answer. And in a broken, barely audible voice she pleads:

"San-ta Mó-ni-ca."

All of them turn rigid, spellbound by the diabolical, shrieking laughter they believe they are hearing and which Isidro was to imitate night after night before an audience that was sitting there with their mouths wide open: "And then the accursed apparition flung herself on us and we felt her stinking flesh touch us, even though I don't believe in things like that, and somebody screamed and that moron of a boss dropped the lamp . . ."

Their fright is tremendous since Santa Mónica is the name of the cemetery. When at last someone manages to light a match, the old woman has vanished and it seems that those nocturnal voices are never going to die down.

Who knows where those damned dogs are roaming now. The next morning Satanas comes out of the thicket and starts howling again. But this howling proclaims Death.

Chapter 25

PUTTING DOWN ROOTS IN MEXICO

I must confess that philosophical treatises have never aroused my curiosity. What's the good in trying to make sense of this world?

But at one time, during my work as an engineer, I happened upon *El Hombre Mediocre* by the Argentine philosopher José Ingenieros. The book itself did not interest me particularly, but I read there a sentence that no doubt motivated me to end my life as a student: "When you unfold your wings and set your inner course toward a distant star to get closer to its sublime light, you carry inside you the mysterious tension of an ideal …"

The star I found for myself was the Taquería Beatríz on Calle Bolívar. My ideal was the sublime beauty of chorizo tacos with guacamole and that mysterious tension was nourished by my ever recurring desire to be able some time to eat as many as I wanted. Indeed, to visit the Taquería Beatríz was one of my passions. But there is no way around the old adage: "A student's sweetheart will never become his wife." These days I can afford any culinary delights I desire, but I have set my course toward different goals. So, adios, Beatríz!

In order to earn money, I spent my vacations during my last four semesters working in a children's home called La Pradera in Cuernavaca. Its owner was Resi Mandl, married to Philip Müller, both of them Social Democrats and refugees from Austria, who had arrived in Mexico before we did and who had helped us out during our first days there.

It was my job to entertain the older children and to help with serving the meals. During the course of this duty, I left a lasting impression when I demonstrated, on general request and during

Doña Resi's absence, how to wolf down four fried eggs in one gulp. I remember these days with the greatest fondness because I was paid well and everybody, including the educators, was pleased I was there. I organized excursions, theatrical performances, and volleyball tournaments, taught swimming, and in the evening told horror stories. For example, the one about the leprous king who replaced those parts of his body he lost to his illness with parts made of gold. These stories were such a resounding success that fifty years later a gray-haired old man berated me for having frightened him for the rest of his life. A short time ago, the wrinkled cashier of a museum thanked me for having taught her how to swim, and an old gentleman with a cane is still angry with me for giving myself first place in a contest of marbles I had organized.

Once during the summer, a group of more than sixty Jewish children from poor families arrived at La Pradera, their vacation paid for by O.S.E. Mexico. These children made me think back to my time in Montmorency near Paris. I think in a certain way I tried to be for these little vacation guests what Günther and John had been for me at Les Tourelles.

On one of the bus trips to Cuernavaca, a young woman and her father – both of them looked like foreigners – sat down behind me and got off like me at the La Pradera stop. I soon found out that the young woman's name was Mathilde Ransenberg, that everybody called her just Mati, and that she too would be working at Resi Mandl's, taking care of the younger children.

My friend Óscar Leal too would now and then take this kind of work I did. Often Mati, Óscar, a tutor from Canada (one of our colleagues), and I went dancing, the *danzón* or *bolero* or we simply walked to the center of Cuernavaca, to the main square with its splendid laurel trees. Those officials who years later ordered a large number of these trees cut down, thereby changing a previously idyllic square into a nondescript place, knew nothing of the value of what they had destroyed forever. To sit there on a bench in the evening's twilight, surrounded by the familiar noise of the *zanates*, aroused a romantic mood, beneficial at least for Mati and me, a romance that gradually turned into love.

On weekends I picked her up at La Pradera to go swimming at Las Estacas, to go for walks, or, when she was in Puebla with her family, to visit her there. In Puebla her parents, Juan Günther and Cecilia, and her younger sister, Mariana, received me with open hearts. It did not take long before I became part of the family's circle of friends.

Juan Günther came from Heimbach, a village on the Rhine near Koblenz. The Ransenbergs were fully integrated into the Jewish community there. At the beginning of the 1930s, Juan Günther owned a printing press he used to run off leaflets opposing the political aims of the Nazis. In 1934, when he tried to bring proscribed literature from Belgium into Germany, he was arrested and sentenced to two and a half years in prison. A short time after his release, he was arrested a second time and sent to the concentration camp at Sachsenhausen. He was married to Cecilia Halfen, who was not Jewish and who was employed by the company where Juan Günther had worked as a courier. The inexhaustible and unrelenting efforts of Cecilia, working together with a group of relatives and friends, led to Juan Günther's release, on the condition that he leave Germany. In Genoa he boarded a ship that took him to Mexico. He settled in Puebla, followed two years later by his wife and their daughters, Mati, eight years old, and Mariana, two. Of the Ransenbergs in Heimbach, only Juan Günther and Grete, one of his sisters, survived the Holocaust. A feeling of guilt for having been chosen for survival stayed with him his whole life.

I felt very much at home with the Ransenbergs, perhaps owing to the similarities in our family history. Juan Günther, like my father, was Jewish; both of them had married a woman of a different faith. But Günther had much closer ties to the Mosaic tradition than my father. I assume that my closeness to this family was one of the reasons that I started to think of Mati as my future wife and as the mother of my children. Five years later, we married in a simple Jewish ceremony.

Mati had an English car that was perhaps suitable for the climate in Britain but certainly not for the heat in the State of Morelos, which we explored from Cuernavaca. We always had to take along a reserve canister of water for the radiator. We drove to Tehuixtla,

With the Ransenbergs in Puebla, about 1956: Bruno, Mati, Dr. Salomon, Mariana (Mati's sister), Father, Mother, Cilli and Juan Günther (Mati's parents)

Palo Bolero, or Cuautla but our favorite place was Las Estacas, which has a river with cold, crystal-clear water. The road we used to get there took us across several creeks and snaked through the sugar-cane fields of Zacatepec. During the harvest, this region was suffused with the sweetish scent of soaking sugar cane and the countryside was stippled with swarms of birds feeding on the insects stirred up by the workers and tractors, amid swaths of gray smoke. I frequently made sketches I used later as motifs for oil paintings.

My passion for the Mexican countryside deepened and bore fruit. Thanks to Mati, herself a painter and excellent at drawing, with her encouragement and stimulation, I was able ten years later on the occasion of an exhibit in San Ángel to experience my first important recognition as a painter.

At that time – at the end of the forties – Las Estacas was a place fully immersed in nature, so completely unspoiled that films with a jungle setting (above all several Tarzan movies) were shot here. Toppled palm trees lay across the pool with mineral springs. One reached the main spring by a trail deeply covered with creepers and occasionally crossed by bright turquoise-colored lizards, salamanders, or snakes. And when we drifted with the current, we could observe large iguanas sunning themselves on the branches above the river or little turtles that hid under the water at the slightest sign of someone approaching. True to my hero, Johnny Weissmuller, I swung across the main pool clinging to a vine that hung down from a high *amate* tree. I was able even at that time to give a perfect imitation of his shout.

Not a year passes even today that I don't drive to Las Estacas at least a few times. I have a fond memory of numerous visits there with my sons, René and Daniel (born in 1955 and 1957), later with my wife, Joan, and more recently with my grandchildren, Renata and Natalia. And even though the original purity and charm of the place have suffered from the modernization of the facility and the throng of people who show up there on weekends with their radios, the number of birds and the strength and clarity of the springs seem to have remained undiminished.

Hardly a year goes by that I don't roam around the countryside near Veracruz. Does this attraction come from the impressions I soaked up during that first bus trip to the capital city? My first favorite place was San Andrés Tuxtla on Lake Catemaco, by whose shore my old friend Antonio Azuela had built a small house. Antonio has often taken me along to the village cantina, where I've always been welcome as Don Bruno. Every evening old friends gather there at their special table, drinking and joshing a great deal, and telling the most unbelievable stories and anecdotes. Yes indeed, the story tellers of San Andrés are famous. Special fame has accrued to the village grocer who starts talking faster and faster whenever a strong north wind threatens. Who can imagine a tapir the size of a cow? A snake that rolls toward its victim like a wheel? Or mud that devours an ox? Inspired by this atmosphere, I wrote the three stories of the following chapters.

Chapter 26

Story

EL SEÑOR LECTOR

When that sojourn in Los Tuxtlas comes back to my mind, I think of the garden in Tebanca, the fragrance of the *guayaba* tree, the teeming mass of scurrying ants in the hollow branch I cracked open. My memory goes back to the dignified elegance of the cranes, the droll antics of the sandpipers, and the spot Isidro pointed out as the best fishing hole.

I see before me the diversity of lush green colors that overwhelm landscape and mind and the volcano that at certain times rises gloomily between storm clouds and that at others can be seen covered with bright stipples of sunlight slowly moving to the rhythm of a strong breeze along the mountainsides. And in the rustle of the winds under the porch roofs where tobacco leaves were hanging to dry, I remember an insistent whisper that I should join the others and listen to them.

He was called El Flaco and turned out to be a veritable hoarder of stories who would without mercy interrupt anybody else's attempt to get a word in edgewise. There was no one who could tell stories about his region the way he could, seeing that he knew it like the pocket of his pants, in all its details, with the deep affection of a person nourished by this huge placenta that never tires of giving: the pastures with I don't know how many heads of cattle per acre and this perpetually moist soil with luxuriant spots of color that lend wonderful accents to this countryside. Even today I marvel full of reverence at how green sprouts can grow out of fence posts one can see along every trail, simple sticks rammed into the ground that turn into trees! And then the apichi leaves grow to such shameless size! All of it in this perennial greenness, constantly pushing upward with life's impetuous, incomprehensible lack of constraint.

El Flaco's cigar factory was located along the way to the waterfall. Gigantic, simple rooms with a jumble of rafters and buttresses under the roof where the tobacco leaves were sorted, unrolled and pressed, an ambience saturated with that strong sweetish scent peculiar to tobacco. The gentle sound of leaves rubbing against each other and the murmur of the workers, all of them women and children. The purring of an engine. Outside one saw the shadows cast by the amate trees with their tremendous roots that let one know something it is impossible to describe precisely: stories in which they lift other trees, walls, foundations with the power of their growth.

But the most fascinating experience still was to see El Flaco turn pensive and start getting into some serious story-telling. Then his eyes would take on a strange radiance, his voice became deeper and he spoke more slowly. That's how I heard him describe the tobacco factory, the way it looked when he was just a little boy and had to fetch the bundles of tobacco leaves from the smoke room. He said that "this job pissed him off royally" because he had to miss a part of Don Plácido's stories who at that time was the man who read to them. El Señor Lector.

From the descriptions El Flaco gave it was not difficult at all to imagine old Don Plácido, sitting in a prominent place with great dignity, dressed in a guayabera shirt and a pair of white linen pants, his Veracruzan hat tilted on his head and a colorful bandana around his neck. The way he carefully cleaned his glasses to guarantee perfect attentiveness. Not until there was nothing but the sound of the chickens cackling and the tobacco leaves rustling would he continue reading at the place where he had stopped the day before. And the workers would listen again to the adventures of Robinson Crusoe, Ali Baba or Don Quixote. It was surely a funny and yet touching experience to see these vivacious children rapturously listening to what happened to Dulcinea del Tobosco or David Copperfield. Don Plácido pulled this amazing feat off. He made the little girls dream of a Snow White lost in mountains where deadly poisonous nauyaca- and corral snakes were lurking. When the Count of Monte Christo was thrown into the sea, the children would surely imagine him being attacked by the sharks and barracudas they were all too familiar with. Heidi's grandfather would no doubt appear to them in the shape of one of the old, raggedy shepherds who roam around in that region. And I am sure, absolutely sure that when Cinderella was dancing with her Prince, a cheerful melody from Veracruz came alive in many little heads.

The heroes of the novels truly took possession of El Señor Lector. During certain passages from *Les Misérables,* he became tightlipped, didn't shave, and barely ate. And when it was D'Artagnan's time to use his skills and wiles against the Cardinal's henchmen, one could see the *chingao* Don Plácido – that's, at any rate, the way El Flaco tells it – on his way home decapitate grasses and bushes with his cane.

When Don Plácido, who was born in nearby Alvarado, would forget his book after a few beers and go on telling the story in his own words, it truly became something worth listening to: "Then the damn stepmother asked the shitty mirror: Mirror, mirror, let me see who the horniest bitch might be in this whole lousy territory."

During the rainy season, all dirt roads turned to mud as creeks swollen into torrents washed the soil off mountains, and swept huts, pigs, chickens away, drowning everything in the murky waters of Lake Catemaco. In times like these, the workers would gather even closer around Don Plácido and, to the hammering sound of the rain on the sheet metal roofs, listen to stories from Dante's *Inferno*.

Throughout many years this was the way the classics were brought to new life. The workers in the tobacco factory had a welcome diversion from the routine of their long hours and they heard stories from a world they would otherwise never have known existed. And at the end of a workday, late in the afternoon, they would gather round the old man and pepper him with questions while they walked home with him on the muddy and by then shaded trails.

But one day the factory was modernized. Not the machines – because work was still done by the dexterous hands of the workers – but by replacing the last reader, Don Plácido, with a radio, with a damn radio, as El Flaco called it.

This happened exactly at the time he had finished reading Selma Lagerlof's *The Coachman of Death*. And the worst thing was that nobody had the courage to tell him beforehand. When he showed up the next morning with a new book, the radio was blasting a dumb serial into the room at full volume.

Don Plácido became ill. Nobody knew what was wrong with him. He was soon forgotten, and the uselessness of his existence began to eat at him. It was said that he thought he was seeing Death around him all the time, sitting on a donkey, lurking in the bushes, or watching him from the holes between the adobe bricks, but usually He appeared to him standing on a coach and grinning at him out of the folds of his hood – as in the novel.

One day Death came to him in the guise of a doctor, and there was no way of escaping Him.

That's how it must have happened. That's how El Flaco tells it.

Sometimes he also tells about how the tobacco plant, because of an epidemic on one of the Caribbean islands, came to Mexico and how healthy plants were brought to this region in order to save the species.

And now I think that it is truly high time to save the few things the epidemic of modernization has not touched as yet.

To a different place. Far away. Into the safety of exile.

Yes, to an island with scissors grinders, street vendors, bird catchers, hurdy-gurdy men, story tellers . . .

And a Señor Lector.

Chapter 27

Story

ANNE BELLE AND THE BIRDS

As every cloudless noon, the sun blazes without mercy, as if it were trying to melt everything. And it comes close to succeeding. The iron of the bench I am sitting on feels red-hot. Wastepaper on the street is turning wavy with a little crackle, and ripples of hot air are rising from the pavement, imparting a touch of motion to the little village square in Veracruz that appears to have ossified. The dogs sit in the shade of *tabachín* trees, panting, and the ice-cream vendor has retreated into the entryway of a house, where he is ringing his little bell in vain because at this time of the day all the people in town take their siesta or try to catch the little breeze they get from their fans as they drink their coffee. The droning air conditioner in the pharmacy, the only one in this whole area, is running on "high." A bumblebee circles me very, very slowly and even the ants, usually so busy, have vanished from this part of the world that is as hot as a crucible.

Would Anne Belle have come out of her home in this heat? At precisely two o'clock, the way people tell it? Dressed all in white? … With her parasol?

A solitary *picho* takes off sluggishly, barely making it to a nearby branch. Then it hops around between a few wilted flowers and across parched patches of grass that have been stamped on by too many shoes. It lifts its tail and adds its share to the bird droppings covering every part of the paved promenade that generations of village beauties in their high-heeled shoes from Paris, that callused soles, huaraches, and hobnailed boots have worn down. A sparrow, numbed by the heat like everyone else and with its beak open, alights on one of the iron benches whose lion claws have been pissed on a hundred times – a relic from a more romantic time in the past.

Did she always make her appearance on time, the crazy woman? She must have walked along this sun-drenched, dusty park trail, her dress touching that low ornate fence that in some places is still completely undamaged.

And over there a bust of Benito Juárez is soaking up the sun, trying to fill an empty spot between the laurel trees. The monument most likely owes its existence to the enthusiasm of a patriotic mayor and quite obviously is the favorite meeting place of all the birds in this village, though it's hard to say where they may have congregated at this moment. In years gone by, its well-bespattered pedestal bore, quite democratically, such diverse heads as those of Garibaldi, Don Porfirio Diaz, and President Calles. And, even farther in the past, Balzac's bust, which had been donated by a romantic devotee of French culture but had never been accorded the kind of high regard it deserved. No doubt all these predecessors of Don Benito were likewise used as the birds' general meeting place.

The town hall, whose dignity is insulted by windows and balconies in need of repairs, is a venue for some apathetic turtledoves to look down on the pervasive lack of activity. Across from it stands the short church tower whose clock, though rusted, still shows the exact time. The bells bear the proud inscription: "Sarignac et Fils, Dijon, 1870." They toll the community's sleepy rhythm every quarter hour.

Half past one . . . The pigeons on the bell tower do not even move. A frazzled *tórtola* flutters back and forth between the pharmacy and the *casa de la loca*. How dignified this house shoulders its years and how regal it looks in the act! The door knocker – a dragon's head struck so many times in the past – on the entrance gate, a portal carved out of zapote wood, resounds through the long hallways, its summons still imperious, and the cast-iron hinges still creak with their accustomed intensity.

The old custodian lets me in, he who knows everything, who has known Anne Belle, the crazy Frenchwoman, and the stories about her.

Time has left its traces everywhere. Worm-eaten salon furniture retains memories of deep sighs beneath its layer of dust. Columns touched by many hands seem to lament past tragedies. Artfully crafted window grates relate scenes from amorous romances. Massive stone walls, vaults, and roof tiles from Marseille speak of a bygone splendor.

The old man tells me that only French was spoken in the house of the crazy woman and that it had been a refuge for persecuted monarchists during the Juárez government, including the petite Frenchwoman, a society lady pampered by "oncle Max et tante Charlotte." She had experienced the tragedy of the two monarchs first hand and had educated her daughter, Anne Belle, in remembrance of those imperial times.

Nearly all the rooms are secured with large padlocks. The only ones open to a curious visitor like me are a bedroom and the main salon. The long hallways are covered with stone tiles from Toulouse. Timber rafters support the stucco-decorated ceilings. Wallpaper with Parisian motifs, moth-eaten. Delicate wood carvings and brocade fabrics covered with yellowed linen sheets. Gloomy paintings and in an easily visible place a life-size portrait of the Emperor Maximilian, lovingly surrounded by a gilded fleur-de-lys frame. In the inner courtyard, the old custodian has hung up his laundry to dry in the sun. A small tip and the little door inside the entrance gate closes behind me.

The clock on the bell tower strikes two.

A lone motorcycle tears the quiet apart like a machine gun. I am too languid to follow it with my eyes, the glare from its metal almost blinding me. Seconds later, the suffocating stillness has returned to the square.

The gate of the large house opens and Anne Belle appears. She is immediately surrounded by a live cloud. More and more birds emerge from the leafy laurel tree, come down from the roofs, cornices, balconies, and lintels, circling round her small, gentle figure. The old lady scatters birdseed among their noisy hubbub. She takes very slow steps, wrapped in a long dress with a train. A graceful parasol, draped with airy little silk kerchiefs, gives her protection. Leaning on her cane, she crosses the street scattering seeds as she moves along. "Mangez, mes petites! . . . You know what you have to do!" Hundreds, nay thousands of wings flutter round the woman: white, black, green with brown, gray, speckled, wings. The sun's light intensifies this dazzling apparition. She seems to be gliding along, suffused with a radiance that seems unreal, as if she had stepped out of a painting by Manet. The silk, the brocade, the ribbons in her hair evoke a France of the bygone century.

But if one takes a closer look, the parasol shows large splotches of mildew. The silk kerchiefs that once adorned it, now hang down faded, and in tatters. The fabric of the flowers on her chapeau is tattered and her veil has holes, hair ribbons with stains and a well-worn neckband. The wrinkled face with small, lively blue eyes, covered with a veil and a thick layer of powder, exudes a hint of trembling gracefulness through the tulle, a spectral apparition. She gives the impression of having lived through a hundred years, through the rain, the heat, the revolutions, love affairs, aging and gradually shrinking but without losing her aristocratic dignity. She suffers the heat with composure and proceeds to the Juárez monument where at last she stops.

And now one can hear the vilest kind of swear words, ejaculated in a soft, hoarse voice with a French accent, issuing from behind a tulle veil through wrinkled lips that have been painted a garish red. Anne Belle proclaims that this is exactly what this Indio deserves: to be forever exposed there to the sun and to be soiled by the birds, her friends. Her neck frill trembles as she exclaims all these deprecations.

The fluttering of wings drowns out the crazy woman's laughter as she shuffles back to her house. "Allez, mes petites . . . You know what you have to do!"

Shortly before she locks the gate behind her, she once more stirs up the flock of birds with her cane. A large, gray, noisy cloud rises and for a moment covers the square in darkness.

A storm cloud has gathered across the sky. The clock has struck 2:15. Only the pigeons nesting in the bell tower, the sparrow on its bench, the humming bumble bee, and the heat are left on the square.

Chapter 28

Story

THE DOCTOR

It was one of those shadeless late mornings that can quickly turn cool. The doctor tried to find the best possible way to proceed while bypassing a stretch of the trail that had turned into deep mud. The ox he was riding trotted up a slippery path, forcing the animal to stop frequently before it could regain its footing. When they had reached the top, the ox took a breather while its rider wrapped a raincoat around himself. It hadn't really started dribbling yet, but the sky, looking like a low-hanging leaden roof, was announcing an imminent downpour. The anticipated storm did not worry the doctor since he was used to torrential rains at this time of the year. Even though there had only been scattered showers during the past few days, he knew that the rainy season wasn't over quite yet. Then the trail would be repaired, as every year. And as always, people would quickly forget how dangerous it had been during the rains.

He turned around to check how far they had come. San Andrés was already far in the distance. Looking past the trees, he was able to recognize a few houses outside the village, and for a few moments he could see some of the ranchos along the slope of the volcano which rose behind the rain clouds, grim and gloomy. Cattle were grazing peacefully amid a following of white cranes. Everything looked shiny as if it had been covered with a thin film of wax. The trail, passing along pasture fences and huge *amate* trees, went through bright-green clearings before its reddish trace disappeared in the woods. This trail, close to ten miles long, was the only connection between San Andrés and Santiago Tuxtla.

From Santiago, it continued in a northerly direction to Lerdo and Alvarado; its southern extension went to Acayucan.

After a while, *ceiba* and *amate* trees flanking his way, the doctor turned off onto a narrow path that was leading to the rancho where they were expecting him. He had been living in this area for many years, and this wasn't the first time he had found himself in a dense jungle during a threatening norther.

This morning he had set out on his horse. But since his mount had slipped repeatedly, he decided to ride to a rancho and exchange it for an ox. They had improvised a semblance of a saddle and bridle using a sweat cloth, sacks, and a belt. Riding an ox would be more cumbersome and take longer, but the doctor didn't want to take chances. No one would take the brewing thunderstorm lightly.

He considered it a privilege every time he was free to force his way through the rain forest. The slow trot of the ox made it possible for him to absorb the atmosphere of the jungle to its full extent, to take in the distant noise of a group of howling monkeys. Familiar sounds were all around him: the croaking of large frogs, the chirping and squealing, the mysterious cracking in the bushes. In a few places, the jungle turned into an inundated clearing where gigantic toppled trees took their time rotting. He enjoyed these rides to make house calls because they afforded him an opportunity to be alone with himself and his memories for a good while: "Oh, you know, doctor, I'll definitely pay next month after the corn harvest" . . . "Now listen, you old quack! Let's see if you really have that steady hand everybody is talking about. So you better fix me up once and for all!" But his memories vanished as soon as he heard a pheasant's squawk coming out of the thicket or a *mazate* fleeing or a flock of birds flying by, their screams announcing the norther.

He estimated that it would be early afternoon before he got to the rancho to start the birthing process. Then some cheerful toasts and a good dinner. Perhaps they'd serve *tepexcuintle*. He smiled to himself.

Although the trail was overgrown with thorny tendrils and some stubborn plants, it wasn't necessary to guide the ox. Huge *apichi* leaves shook when the animal's body brushed against them. A slap with the cane now and then perked up its trot.

A dog walked with them. It was one of those bellicose village curs that often followed the doctor on his rides. A tough mutt that was used to being outside in any weather. It ran back and forth, sniffed and pissed incessantly, chased the cranes, *chacalacas* and squirrels.

As soon as the first drops fell, the dog's hunting zeal was gone. He started trotting along close to the ox. The clouds became heavier and heavier. Protected by his rain coat, the rider leaned into the breaking storm. The dog, its ears no longer pricked up, put his tail between his legs and stayed even closer to the ox who continued plodding up one hill and down the next through reeds and muddy creeks. These hadn't been there a short time ago. A little later the rain slowed somewhat. The man shook the water from his coat, relaxed and thus was able to smell the scent of rotting plants that the rain had intensified.

When he came to a normally small creek, he was surprised to find it swollen to many times its usual depth. "So what will the river look like? . . . Certainly dangerous . . . But with an ox there won't be a problem," he thought. Crossing the creek wasn't easy because a piece of the bank on the other side had broken off. The animal slid and fell on its side. The doctor's bag dropped into the morass. He needed to get the ox on its feet and gather his things. Then he climbed back into the saddle, angry and covered in mud. All of a sudden, the rain stopped completely, followed by silence all around, which the doctor was unable to enjoy this time. He was worried about crossing the river.

Then the storm broke. A series of thunderclaps and lightning flashes struck the volcano. As suddenly as the rains had stopped, water now was pouring from the sky again. Squalls swept across the jungle, bending everything to the ground, tearing up the leaves and tossing large branches through the air. The trail was barely recognizable any longer, torrents everywhere. The doctor had a brief vision of his own house. Go back? It was too late for that. And if there were complications with the birth? He had to keep going.

The ox continued on its way, though its steps were getting slower and slower. There was no use trying to prod the beast. The dog trotted by its side, crouched low, a wet rag.

The doctor took a few sips of brandy and thought about the impenetrability of the jungle during the rainy season. He felt tired.

"Why don't you just take it easy, Doc!" He owned a small rancho on Lake Catemaco. Yes, why not, finally? Then he wouldn't have to be out here in this infernal weather . . . "Look, mother, how beautifully our *almendro* tree is coming along!" . . . "Pick me some oranges, grandpa!" It was the first time that thoughts like these had run through his mind.

The trail had disappeared beneath masses of mud and torn-off branches, the animal using all the strength at its command to force its way through them. The doctor tried to imagine how he might make it to the rancho safely. But his worries about crossing the river wouldn't go away.

When he got there, he was surprised to see that the river was not carrying as much water as he had feared. The rainfall up there at the foot of the volcano had probably not been as intense. An uprooted tree was blocking part of the river bed. The dog started barking and yowling.

The dog's howling alarmed the doctor. He had never heard him moaning like this before. But there was no way to turn back. He had to get across! He looked for a suitable place and urged the ox on. It took a few steps and then just stopped, snorting, shaking all over, starting to bellow, and trying to turn back. The doctor managed even so to push the animal to keep moving. It slowly started crossing the river, water reaching as high as the saddle. With a sudden roar, the raging current carried the ox along a few yards. Trying to find some ground, its forelegs got stuck in the mud that had slid off the embankment. The ox was sinking in almost to its neck while the doctor kept lashing it. He tried to keep a clear head, to find a solution. But what could he do? Throw himself into this mud? He thought of his family.

"Will you be back tomorrow, grandpa?" . . . "Take care of yourself, Papa!" The churned-up masses of slime and mud and the image of them engulfing his body addled his thinking.

He had to get through this! Get this damn ox to move forward! He screamed as he kicked his heels into the animal's sides. But the ox was no longer able to move, as it desperately tried to fight off the mud getting into his snout and ears, while it sank deeper and deeper. Its movements slowed, and finally it stopped moving altogether. His strength giving out, the doctor clung to the drowning animal. The last thing he heard was the thundering storm and very far away, through roaring sheets of rain, the moaning yowls of the dog.

The wind turned and the storm's fury diminished over the last few hours. The campesinos found the doctor, clinging to the ox. The dog, bewildered, came crawling out of a hollow tree. The jungle had regained its calm, a gentle rustle of the trees, the sound of invisible birds. The piercing noise of the cicadas seemed never to have stopped. The river kept flowing without commotion. Cranes and herons were pecking in the mud, birds of prey circling high above in a gloomy sky, down below a cloud of mosquitoes buzzing around everything that protruded from the morass. The men crossed themselves.

And while the muck was slowly squeezing all life out of the doctor, a newborn baby nearby was holding onto its own life.

Chapter 29

THE DECISION

There was a rumor circulating among the handful of students majoring in communications at the beginning of the 1950s that the newly founded television station was looking for young engineers with college diplomas. Who could have predicted the advances this industry would make from then on? In November of 1950, I joined the technical staff of Latin America's first television network. I was made chief of maintenance. Maintenance? Me? The one with the two left hands? When I showed up for work, in suit and tie as was appropriate for a young engineer, the technical director quickly made me face facts. He had me install shock absorbers on the turntables since their needles would regularly jump out of their grooves every time the rather portly technician passed by. In my mind, I put myself in the hand of Tin-Tan (my carpentry teacher at the vocational school), took off my tie, and went to work.

All installations operated with vacuum tubes. What nowadays is accommodated on a dime-size chip in those days required the space of an armoire. Even though our equipment was new, it often failed. The classical method of locating the source of a failure was to knock on all tubes until one found the trouble spot.

Our studio occupied an area slightly larger than fifteen by fifteen yards. In this limited space all kinds of programs were recorded, from the news through horror serials, from plays to *zarzuelas*. During one of these recording sessions, the orchestra had to be seated on two platforms. The musicians on the upper deck were sitting so close to the spotlights that their violin bows were moving up and down between the lamps while the players sweated as if they were in a sauna, and they constantly had to retune their instruments. These programs were directed by Brígida Alexander, an actress who had come to Mexico as a refugee and with whom I was to develop a close friendship that endured for decades.

Even though I was officially responsible for maintenance, I had to perform every kind of job, as did all the others too. Once I substituted for a technician who was in charge of the camera images. The program was called *The Threshold of Terror* and started with a shot of a gloomy castle gate opening to allow the appearance of the butler. Some part of the camera was not working right and produced a strange effect, changing from negative to positive, as the picture slowly turned. The producer was enthusiastic and shouted that this was the most spectacular thing he had ever seen, insisting that I should repeat it in the next episode.

In those early years of television, the technology of video recordings was unknown. Video tapes were not invented until eight years later when the Ampex Company developed them in the United States. Every production was broadcast the way it was filmed in the studio.

A program by Teatro de Manolo Fábregas was about a jealous baker who stuffs his wife's lovers into the oven (perhaps inspired by the French movie, *La femme du boulanger)*. At the dramatic climax, the baker hoists his final victim on his shoulders, huffing and puffing as he opens the oven door from which flames are belching – at least according to the script. Instead, the prop assistant was looking out of the opening and wanted to know if it was time for the flames to come out.

Brígida Alexander (she died in 1998) was in charge of one of the first series on Latin American television: "Angeles de la calle" (Street Angels). The outdoor scenes were filmed among street vendors near the area where the newspapers were printed. In one scene when the villain strikes one of the newsboys, pedestrians tried to interfere, assuming that this was a genuine altercation. The little episode was broadcast live, with me in the midst of things trying to calm everybody down. That was my debut as a television actor – an activity I continued to pursue years later in horror serials or soap operas, frequently in the role of the doctor who broke the news of her fatal illness to the heroine against a background of dramatic music. At any rate, these live broadcasts simulated reality, making it look authentic in a way that in the years to come was

As a camera man in the studio of Canal 4,
Mexico City, 1952

hardly ever surpassed by prerecorded programs.

Work at Televisa, an organization of world renown, was an adventure for me that ended only with my retirement in 1998. Its *telenovelas* (soap operas) and serials were shown in more than a hundred countries. Recently, my wife was informed by friends in South Africa that they had been surprised to see me in the serial *The Shadow,* in which I played an evil doctor.

I have always made sure not to let my activities as an actor limit my technical work. And what's more, my superiors hardly ever knew of my "other" activities. During the 1980s, when I was one of the technical directors of the network, I tested, in the presence of my boss, the quality of transmission via a satellite from the United States. When the connection was established at last, everybody was greatly surprised when I appeared on the screen the moment I was being shot to death by Colombian soldiers. It was a scene from the film *Green Ice*, which had been made in Mexico a few years before, with my participation. For a while, the joke was circulating that Schwebel the engineer had a twin brother who was an actor.

In those years, my real brother frequently changed jobs, girl friends, and cars, the last fact making me quite envious. Today, as I write these recollections, he is no longer alive. I think of his life with its ups and downs, a life in large part dedicated to women's fashion. In a certain sense, he had adjusted to Mexico better than I. In contrast to me, he never thought that he might return to Austria; he also had never been interested in finding a wife whose background was similar to ours. In 1953 he married Conchita, a loveable and gentle woman who gave him his two daughters, Pati and Nora. Later he wed a pretty model, Lupita, and then Ofelia, who nursed him until his death in 2001. With her he had a son, Allan.

At the beginning of the fifties, we moved to the southern part of town. My father took over Max Diamant's delicatessen when Max decided to return to Germany, where he was to work with Willy Brandt. The new store was located across from Parque España, not far from our previous shop, so that my father did not lose his regular customers. Business was good, even though I would stop by before going to work and load up on goodies for supper: a huge sandwich filled with ham, salami, cheese, little onions, and gherkins and a second one of the same kind for the moochers among my colleagues. Evil tongues maintain that these lootings brought about my father's ruin.

In reality, though, Papa was completely in the wrong place for this line of work. I still see him behind the counter, solving crossword puzzles between customers or reading the *Arbeiterzeitung*, with a touch of wistfulness in his face and perhaps envy that Max Diamant could return to the political life of his native country. True, he seemed to be in good spirits, but jokes like "My Kraków sausages just arrived from Poland" or "The Limburg cheese stinks better than ever before, madam," had lost their former punch. Ten years of fighting with headstrong customers and wholesalers, with every sort of inspector and beggar, had worn him out. When he showed signs of impatience with his most loyal customers, we knew it was time for him to look for a different occupation.

Somebody convinced him to buy an Italian pasta machine and to offer its products, macaroni and spaghetti, to restaurants and groceries. He sold his store to his assistant, Chucho, who didn't hesitate to turn this respected shop into a taco and torta shack.

Father in his shop, Mexico City, 1955

But how hard Papa struggled with that piece of mechanical nonsense! Even though it ran on electricity, its frequent failures forced him to operate its crank by hand, and he would often come home exhausted and in a foul mood. In the end he sold the machine and spent the rest of his life selling my mother's fancy cakes along with the honey and the Gelée Royal that Swiss friends produced.

My father died in 1975 of a kidney disease that caused him to suffer from periods of confusion. In his last days, he saw Gestapo agents standing in the door of his room. "Look, look, there they are again!" he would say to me, upset and speaking Viennese. "No, Papi, don't be afraid, we're in Mexico and safe," I'd answer him.

After Father's death, my mother started to make repeated trips to Austria. She spent several weeks with relatives, above all with her sister-in-law, Hanni, or her niece, Meli. But she was always happy to return to Mexico, to her sons, grandchildren, and friends and to her opera evenings at the Palacio de Bellas Artes. She died in 1981. My parents and my brother are buried in the Israelite Cemetery of

Mother as a pastry baker, advertisement from the 1960s

Mexico City.

In 1953 I passed my state exams in electronics and communication. Soon thereafter the Austrian government certified me as an "engineer," which gave me permission to work in this profession in my native country.

Just as I had at the end of the war, I thought again about returning to Austria. That homesickness I had felt eight years ago was undiminished, and I had begun to analyze the anger with which I looked at my fellow countrymen though I was far from having overcome it. But no. I had put down roots by now, I felt good, and a splendid future lay ahead of me. That was the moment I decided to get married, to have children and to lead my life in Mexico, a country which had granted us asylum a dozen years ago.

Chapter 30

RETURNING

Whenever I visit Austria I feel an urge to return to the places of my childhood. I think of them long before the start of every trip back. Except for the one in 2002, nearly all my sojourns were of short duration, which is the reason I always return to Mexico frustrated: I had not seen everything, truly everything once more. It does indeed take some time to become clear about one's feelings and to unravel recollections, and giving free rein to one's bottled-up emotions seems to call for an unending effort. Most people living in exile have the same experience. I know that.

On my first return, sixteen years after our flight, Mati accompanied me. First I drove to Neulengbach, walked up the path to the Haaghof, entered grandfather's orchard, sat down, and started crying.

During later visits, however, I began to feel my tenseness loosening. Each time the Haaghof had been renovated a little more. One day I found the garden subdivided into lots, with a half-finished house on one of them. Once again a family had pushed its way in, strangers with an unfriendly look in their eyes.

Intuitively I felt robbed of what belonged to me. With bitterness I observed the new residents and thought about how they would react if I were to tell them something about the past, about this house and the Jewish family who had lived there for twenty years. Would they be afraid that I might take legal steps to reclaim this property? I think of my grandfather, of his last days at the Haaghof, alone with his daughter, Helene. What had happened on that day in September of 1939, when he had to resign himself to being taken to a home for the aged on Seegasse in Vienna? Did he believe, full of hope, that his family had found safety in another country?

At the same time, I am drawn back again and again to the house in which the old Hössingers lived, Mama's parents. I have walked past the railroad depots where we were forbidden to play as children or past the former brickworks or I sit under the chestnut trees across from the station, at the tavern where Grandpa and his cronies would get together. When I see the old men drinking their beer, it crosses my mind that one of them could possibly have been a classmate of mine and I imagine his face if I were to ask him about this. Would he recognize in me the little boy who behaved so differently during the daily "Our Father?" I also think what's past is past, but what would have become of me? A railroad official, like so many of them? Driving a locomotive, my dream and that of all the other boys?

I take the dirt road leading to my old school in the center of town, remember that I had walked barefoot and that my feet had hurt sometimes, but that my pride had kept me from whining in front of my brother or my cousin Dita who were walking with me. I took my time, stealing an apple from one of the over-laden trees, kicking stones. I offer to everyone who crosses my path a "Grüß Gott!" and ask myself why these people are so annoyed about returning my brief salutation, and I remember that Mexican villagers always have a friendly word.

My visits to Purkersdorf take a similar course. I walk on the street from our house to the school, ask myself how I was able to cross those tracks with their gates down when those kids were chasing us, throwing rocks, stroll across the old bridge at the Unter-Purkersdorf station, wait until the train has passed through but deny myself the pleasure of dropping a pebble. What would people think of me?

On one occasion, I climbed to the top of Schöffelstein. I was surprised to see the number of signs that make it easier for day trippers to identify mushrooms, animals, and wild plants and to discover how well the trails were marked. The amount of windfall wood lying around, a sign of prosperity, made me wonder if I could still handle those large bundles I had dragged home as a child.

I have made it a habit to walk by the houses where we lived, never noticing any major changes. The swing set on which I played with my cousin Lizzi is still at the same place, and that gate in which my wrist got stuck in 1938 is still the same. I barely recognize Aunt Anni's house without Uncle Rudolf at the window.

Here I think back to the time we said good-bye to my aunt when we took off for France.

On every visit to Vienna, no matter how brief, I try to pass for a local. I hide my camera, speak Viennese, and order my "Bratwuascht" with bread and mustard like any stalwart native. Yet even so, I stop sheepishly in front of pastry-shop displays or succumb, like all tourists, to the magic of the Mozart Orchestra in the hall of the Musikverein. But I do run away from the horse cabs, from the confection known as Mozartkugel, from the shows with the horses, and from the hordes of tourists at Schönbrunn and in Grinzing. I always seek just a little touch of the blue from the Strauss waltz in the brown waters of the Danube and to recapture that old pleasure of spitting from the Nordbahn Bridge, or I discover buildings I'm sure didn't exist in my childhood, while I come away empty-handed from strolling through the Danube meadows looking for paper kites or a pickle vendor.

I'm suspicious, albeit less so with every visit, of the people I observe, looking for friendly glances. On Allerheiligenplatz mothers are still engaged in serious chats while they knit, and the children's games haven't changed. I walk to the Janecek-Hof, climb up to the fourth floor where our apartment was, instinctively counting the steps the way I did as a little boy, and read the name on the neighbor's door – expecting it to be "Frau Bender."

I devour all kinds of dumplings and savor dishes meant only for Austrian palates, such as Krenfleisch, Tafelspitz, or Kaiserschmarrn, presumably the Emperor Franz Joseph's favorite dessert. (A translation of these delicacies would only provoke international culinary conflicts.)

During my visit in 2002, I spent seven weeks in Austria accompanied by my wife, Joan, my dear Joan who has shown so much fascinated interest in my past and in my family's fate and in my own feelings. The major reason for this visit was an invitation from the Mexican Embassy in Vienna and various other institutions, most prominent from the city administration, to participate in a celebration in memory of Mexico's protest against the Anschluß of March 1938. I was to represent the Austrian refugees in Mexico. A further reason was for me to read from my "Recollections" and some of my short stories before literary circles

With Joan at the Danube in Vienna, March 2002

in Vienna, Salzburg, Bad Ischl, and Graz.

This visit led me to change my attitude about Austria and the Austrians markedly. The country that had told me sixty-four years ago: "Get out, Yid, or get killed," this time bade me a cordial welcome. And indeed, I relished having my wounds soothed that way even as I grappled with guilt feelings. This relatively long sojourn also gave me an opportunity to get to know many people more closely. If I were to live in Vienna, I would choose to become part of a circle of friends who would help me in my attempt to join that perhaps small segment of society with whom I share similar values. But I cannot ignore the fact that anti-Semitism, which is said to have deep roots in the Austrian soul, is still in evidence even though there are indications that those roots are losing some of their strength.

At the same time, I succeeded in those seven weeks better than ever before "to play the perfect native of Vienna," even if, in my trips across the city or in the streetcar along the Ring, I did not quite manage to put on the same indifferent look as the other passengers. I was amused to hear the waiter at Café Museum ask me: "Another little espresso, Herr Doktor?" Was he having his fun with me? And it came back to my mind that everybody at the Café Gandhi in Mexico called me Don Bruno. I observed the local chess players during their speed games and was delighted by the outrageous comments of the onlookers. I wanted to be part of it, but somehow it did not work. These groups were not very welcoming. Who is this outsider that he should feel insolent enough to assume he can keep up with us? Even so, I managed to play a few games. The atmosphere at the Gandhi is more open and relaxed. Too bad they don't serve poppy-seed strudel.

In the museums, I joined the Austrians in their patriotic admiration of Schiele, Klimt, Waldmüller, and Hundertwasser. During my latest visit with the Emperor Maximilian at the Kapuzinergruft, the Crypt of the Capuchin Monks, I thought once more what a dreamer he must have been, noticing that his coffin still is raised higher than that of the other emperors – presumably so that its inscription about his having been "murdered" in Mexico could not be read easily – and I warbled "La Paloma," one of his favorite tunes. In the Ethnological Museum I verified for myself that Moctezuma's feather headdress was still in its display case – despite the frequent demonstrations on St. Stephen's Square by Mexican Indios and a few palefaces who amid the rhythms of rattling bells, *teponaxtles* (drums), and the trumpet sounds of gigantic conches demand its return to Mexico.

As Joan and I were walking down Andreas-Hofer-Straße in Floridsdorf, the song "Shackled in Mantua, our loyal Hofer lay," which we had learned in elementary school, came back to me. How much patriotism is expected of me today? The Prince Eugene Monument made me think automatically of "Prinz Eugen, der edle Ritter, foat mim Oasch durchs Fenstergitter" (Prince Eugene, the noble knight, shows his arse in broad daylight), and while crossing Radetzky Square on my way to the Prater, I hummed to myself "When the dog jumps the fence with a bone in his snout," a popular version of the Radetzky March from my childhood.

On my way back to the bus that was to take me up the Kahlenberg, I found myself on Twelfth of February Square, opposite Karl-Marx-Hof, that municipal block of tenements I hadn't seen since 1934. I remember when I had gone there with my father, remember his worried expression and the holes in the walls. The square, a well-tended park today, had been full of debris. I am sure I was afraid. Did I cling to my mother's hand or my father's leg? I was surprised that the names of the square and of the buildings whose significance not many Viennese know have survived all the changes of governments and politics.

All over Vienna, poster advertisements could be seen using the old children's game "I spy" as their slogan. I too had played this game as a child, but through this advertising campaign, I saw something nobody else did: red flags with swastikas hanging from every building. And I realized that in spite of my many visits I was unable to separate these places from their past or this past from certain people I encountered on the streets. I don't know how many Nazis are still alive, but it is known that for every four hundred Viennese there is only one Jew and it makes me sad that Jews prefer to keep their background a secret.

Before I returned to Mexico, Joan and I went up the Leopoldsberg because we wanted to enjoy a bird's-eye view of Vienna and then to walk down to Kahlenbergdorf. I tried to imagine this landscape as painted by Kokoschka and how I would paint it. The morning mist hovering across the city reminded me of Mexico City suffocating under smog. A memorial plaque in honor of the thousands of Austrians whom the Soviet occupation troops at the end of the war had sent to Siberia as slaves brought me back to reality. It is true – nobody had really been spared by the war! I took

With grandchildren, Natalia and Renata, Mexico City, 2001

a deep breath and, as we were walking down, I stopped at a lilac bush to enjoy its barely perceptible fragrance. I wondered why this bush didn't also grow in Mexico, and then I thought of my mother and broke off a twig.

Notes

Chapter 1

Gachupines — a derogatory term for Mexico's colonial Spaniards, the *Peninsulares*.

National holiday — to celebrate the proclamation of independence (the so-called *Grito de Dolores*) on September 16, 1810.

Janecek-Hof — the largest of "Red Vienna's" major municipal housing projects of the mid-1920s, comprising 841 apartments and five inner courtyards; built in 1925/26 and named after Johann Janecek (1881-1932), a local Social Democratic administrator and a prominent trade unionist.

Handelskai — an industrial road in Vienna along the southern bank of the Danube.

February 1934 — on February 12, confrontations between armed formations of the Social Democrats, the *Republikanische Schutzbund* (Republican Protective League), on the one side, and the *Heimwehr*, the military arm of the Christian Socials and of the federal government under Chancellor Engelbert Dollfuß, on the other, escalated into four days of bloody civil war. Fighting started in Linz when members of the *Heimwehr*, acting as auxiliary police, tried to disarm members of the *Schutzbund* and confiscate their weapons. Their resistance immediately brought about a militant uprising in several industrial centers, especially in the working-class districts of Vienna. These acts of armed opposition met with massive artillery attacks and were put down ruthlessly, leading to nearly 200 deaths and over 300 injured among the leftists; government losses were 128 dead and 409 wounded. The uprising, a determined though desperate response to frequent provocations, was poorly organized;

it was doomed to failure when the Social Democrats' call for a general strike found little popular support. Some revolutionary leaders were executed, others – among them Julius Deutsch and Otto Bauer – fled into exile. Their party, as well as all trade unions and socialist workers' organizations were outlawed. On May 1, 1934, a new, authoritarian constitution with a one-party system (*Ständestaat*) was ratified. It replaced all political parties with interest groups representing the traditional economic and professional interests of the country, the *Vaterländische Front*, thereby legalizing the program of Austro-Fascism.

Grinzing — a historic village at Vienna's northern periphery, since 1891 a part of Döbling, the XIXth District.

Kahlenberg — at 1468 ft., one of Vienna's favorite destinations for day trips.

Galicia — area north of the Carpathian Mountains comprising the southern parts of Poland and the Ukraine; until 1918, the largest eastern crown land of the Austro-Hungarian monarchy with a population in 1910 of 7.3 million, of whom less than 3% spoke German.

Petlyura — Simon Vasilyevich Petlyura (1878-1926), a nationalist Ukrainian politician. He was Minister of War in 1917 and then chairman of the Directorate that governed the Ukrainian People's Republic, in which capacity he instigated anti-Jewish pogroms between 1918 and 1920.

Chapter 2

Schiele — Egon Schiele (1890-1918), expressionist painter of landscapes and portraits, often of nudes, that were frequently denounced as pornographic.

Plague — the epidemic of 1679 killed close to 50,000 people.

Siege — the desperate defense of Vienna against an overwhelming Turkish force under Kara Mustafa ended in victory when an army of 70,000 under the Polish king John Sobieski broke the siege of a city that was about to surrender.

Chapter 3

Robert Streibel — *Februar in der Provinz* (Grünbach: Verlag Franz Steinmaßl, 1994).

Hannerl — *Singspiel* in three acts, score by Franz Schubert, arranged by Carl Lafite; Libretto by Alfred Maria Willner and Heinz Reichert. (Vienna, 1918).

Willner (1859-1929) and Reichert (1877-1940 in Los Angeles) — who frequently collaborated, were both very successful writers of operetta libretti.

On Orders from the Duchess — operetta in three acts by Bruno Granichstaedten (1879-1944, New York), libretto by Leopold Jacobson and Robert Bodanzky; first performed at the Theater an der Wien on March 20, 1915.

The Lucky Girl — operetta in three acts by Robert Stolz (1880-1975, between 1938 and 1946 in the United States), first performed at the Raimundtheater in Vienna and quickly a great international success, in the United States as *Sky High*. Stolz composed 51 operettas and musicals, nearly 100 movie scores, and some 1200 songs.

Volkswacht — Social Democratic weekly, published 1918-1934.

Wetzlas — in the Waldviertel near Zwettl, some fifty miles northwest of Vienna.

Chapter 4

Vichy — France's most luxurious spa, in the Allier Department, 28 miles north-northeast of Clermont-Ferrand. In July 1940, Vichy became the seat of the conservative-collaborationist government under Marshal Henri Philippe Pétain (1856-1951), who concluded the armistice with Hitler. Though never more than nominally independent but not an abject puppet regime either, his administration was given nearly absolute power to rule the unoccupied southern 40% of the country according to German instructions. With the deployment of German troops to the South after the Allied invasion of North Africa in November 1942, Vichy's minimal autonomy was revoked. Its legitimacy officially ended with the establishment of a provisional government under Charles de Gaulle on August 25, 1944.

Zakopane — a center of alpine sports and tourism in the Tatra Mountains of Poland, some fifty miles south of Kraków.

Maximilian — Ferdinand Maximilian (1832 in Vienna – 1867 in Querétaro), the younger brother of the emperor Francis Joseph I. In 1863 he was chosen by a group of Mexican exiles and Napoleon III of France to replace Benito Juárez, the president of the Republic of Mexico. He accepted the Mexican throne on April 10, 1864, when he was guaranteed the protection of a French army for six years. Since he lacked political experience, the difficulties he encountered soon proved insurmountable. In October 1866, he agreed to abdicate when the French withdrew their troops. Even so, he was persuaded to remain as the leader of some 20,000 Mexican soldiers, who, in May 1867, were forced to surrender. His court-martial and execution after a flurry of diplomatic activities to secure his release were meant to serve as a lesson to foreign interventionists.

Chapter 5

Schöffel — Josef Schöffel (1832-1910), a journalist and politician whose articles in the daily *Wiener Tagblatt* between 1870 and 1872 contributed significantly to saving the Vienna Woods from deforestation.

War of 1866 — the war between Prussia and Austria, ostensibly over the administration of Schleswig-Holstein, which established Prussian dominance in Germany. The decisive defeat of the Austrian army at the Battle of Königgrätz/Sadowa (July 3, 1866) led to the dissolution of the German League and the exclusion of Austria from German affairs.

Hoffmann — Josef Hoffmann (1870-1956), architect and interior designer, professor at the School for Arts and Crafts (Kunstgewerbeschule) in Vienna (1899-1937) and founder (with Koloman Moser) of the Wiener Werkstätte (1903-1932). Prominent among his art-nouveau and art-deco buildings are the Sanitarium in Purkersdorf (1903-1905), the Palais Stoclet in Brussels (1905-1911), and various villas in and around Vienna. He also applied his aesthetic principles to municipal apartment blocks (Klose-Hof, Winarsky-Hof).

Avándaro — popular weekend and tourist destination, south-west of Mexico City.

Dr. Caligari — *Das Kabinett des Dr. Caligari* (1920), a classic of expressionist film, directed by Robert Wiene.

Horst Wessel — the "martyred" Berlin storm trooper Horst Wessel (1907-1930) is said to have written this song in 1927. It became the anthem of the National Socialist (Nazi) movement and was often played together with the official "*Lied der Deutschen.*"

Schuschnigg — Kurt Schuschnigg (1897-1977), Austrian chancellor between 1934 and 1938, who continued the authoritarian form of government established by his predecessor, Engelbert Dollfuß. He forged close ties with Mussolini and propagated Austria as "the second German state," as he tried to secure his country's independence. The plebiscite on this issue did not take place since German troops occupied Austria the day before. Schuschnigg was forced to abdicate on May 11 and was kept under arrest until 1945.

Fabela — Isidro Fabela (1882-1964), Mexican diplomat with many foreign postings, among them as his country's representative to the League of Nations (1937-1940), in which capacity he wrote Mexico's protest against the annexation (*Anschluß*) of Austria by Nazi Germany.

Grynszpan — On November 7, 1938, Herschel Grynszpan (1921-1943) shot the third secretary of the German embassy in Paris, Ernst vom Rath, to protest the deportation of his parents from Hanover to Zbaszyn on the Polish frontier. He was immediately arrested by the French police. On the evening of that same day, Joseph Goebbels, Hitler's Minister for Popular Enlightenment (*Volksaufklärung*), ordered all German newspapers to carry the assassination as front-page news. He also had members of the SA and the SS instigate a pogrom during which more than 2500 synagogues and 7500 businesses were ransacked and numerous Jews were killed.

Chapter 6

Mauthausen — the harshest and largest concentration camp in Austria, covering 37 acres near an abandoned stone quarry in the district of Perg in Upper Austria north of the Danube. It was created shortly after the Annexation and existed until May 5, 1945. At one time it had close to fifty satellite camps. Its first prisoners were 3,833 German criminals and other "asocial" and "undesirable political elements" who had been transferred from Dachau. The total number of prisoners who passed through Mauthausen is estimated to have been 200,000 (335, 000 for the entire system), of whom 119,000 died, among them 38,120 Jews. The highest number of prisoners who passed through Mauthausen was 114,524 in 1944, among them 65,645 new prisoners, including 13,826 Jews, of whom 3437 died. At the time of the camp's liberation, there were 84,000 inmates at Mauthausen, Poles constituting the largest national group. See *Encyclopedia of the Holocaust,* Israel Gutman, general editor, vol. 3 (New York, London: Macmillan, 1990).

Chapter 7

Stern — Josef Luitpold Stern (1886-1966), a Viennese journalist and poet who, during the first Republic (1919-1934), was a prominent organizer of the city's adult education and library system. He administered the Center for Workers' Education (1919-1926) and served as the director of its Workers' University in Wien-Döbling (1926-1934). During his four years of exile in Brno (Brünn), Czechoslovakia, until 1938 and then in Paris and southern France, he published his poetry in the *Hundert Hefte*, brochures of 32 pages each, at his own expense. During his years in the United States (September 2, 1940, until May 1, 1948), he was employed as a social worker at Pendle Hill, a Quaker Settlement for Negroes near Philadelphia, and as an assistant librarian in its College Settlement, where he edited six (of his altogether seventy) *Hefte*. After his return to Vienna, he served as the president (*Rektor*) of the *Arbeiterhochschule* (Workers' College) in Weinberg, Upper Austria. From 1954 until 1959, he headed the commission on education of the Austrian League of Trade Unions (*Gewerkschaftsbund*) in Vienna.

Piaf — Edith Gassion (1913-1963), popularly known as "Piaf" (sparrow), actress and singer, who was famous for her renditions of the Parisian chanson.

Kindertransporte — a program to evacuate some 20,000 Jewish children from Germany, Austria, and Czechoslovakia in order to save them from Nazi persecution. The largest number of them were sent to Great Britain – a total of 9,354 according to the Refugee Children's Movement (RCM) – the first transport arriving at the port of Harwich on December 2, 1938. The program was suspended at the outbreak of war on September 1, 1939. Criteria for selection were stringent: to be accepted, the children had to be at least two years old but not older than seventeen, travel unaccompanied, and have no psychological or medical problems that might endanger their inconspicuous and rapid assimilation to a different way of life. A deposit of fifty pounds was required, a guarantee usually provided by Jewish aid committees in England. The younger children were placed in private foster homes, the older ones in hostels and similar institutions. Their schooling ended after they turned fourteen, when they were trained for work in agriculture, offices, or households. Many of these so-called "transmigrants" volunteered for military service; about 60% became British subjects. Most of them never saw their parents again.

Marianne Pollak (1891-1963) — a teacher of English and French, a journalist, and a politician, who lived in exile (in Switzerland, Brussels, Paris, and London) from 1934 until 1945. Shortly after her return to Vienna in 1945, she was elected to the National Council (*Nationalrat*), Austria's lower house of parliament. She served until 1959 as a member of the Socialist Party (SPÖ), most prominently as an advocate of the women's movement.

Red Falcons — a worldwide organization for children aged 12 to 14, sponsored in this case by the Social Democratic Party of France.

Prestataire étranger — a member of various auxiliary units that, beginning in April 1939, were recruited from foreign workers and attached to companies of the French army.

Chapter 8

O.S.E. (Oeuvre de Secours aux Enfants) — a Jewish aid organization for children that in 1939 operated four homes north of Paris: two in Montmorency with 150 beds, La Chaisnaie in Eaubonne with 70 beds, the villa Les Tourelles in Soissy, and La Guette, the refuge of orthodox Jews. By June of 1940, some 1,600 children, three to fifteen years old, were being cared for in twelve homes in France. Their chief financial sponsors were the Baroness Pierre de Gunzbourg and Baron Guy de Rothschild. See: Hillel J. Kieval, "Legality and Resistance in Vichy France: The Rescue of Jewish Children," *Proceedings of the American Philosophical Society*, vol. 124, no. 5 (October 1980): 339-366.

Ernst Papanek (1900-1973) — a member of Austria's Social Democratic Workers' Party (SDAP) and a prominent advocate of school reform. In February 1934, he had to flee to Czechoslovakia, where, until 1938, he organized the exiles' opposition against Austrian fascism. In Paris, he administered the O.S.E. homes, an activity about which he reports in his book, *Out of the Fire* (New York: Morrow, 1975). After the fall of France, he and his family emigrated to the United States, where he was employed first as a social worker and, from 1949 until 1958, as the principal of the Wiltwych School for Boys in New York, an institution for juveniles with a criminal record. Thereafter, he taught pedagogy at Queens College – without, however, being able to implement his educational theories about the communal socialization of troubled children.

Käthe Bodek — a social worker in Germany and in Spain during the Civil War. The typescript of her unpublished memoirs, written in 1950, circulated among friends.

St. Louis — a luxurious cruise ship of the Hamburg-America Line (Hapag) that was chartered by a group of wealthy German Jews to take 937 passengers to Cuba, where they were to wait for their visas to enter the United States as immigrants. Even though their travel and residence documents were in perfect order, the Cuban authorities reneged on their assurances. Urgent appeals to their

American counterparts proved equally futile. In May of 1939, the St. Louis was forced to return to Europe, where her passengers, after a journey of 33 days, disembarked at ports along the English Channel.

Chapter 9

Montintin — an estate in the village of Château Chervix, about forty miles from Limoges. The fee for the use of the property was 40,000 francs.

Sauf-conduit — a certificate of safe passage issued to refugees for travel within and through France. Visas could be obtained only at consulates in Nice and Marseille. Between mid-May and mid-June of 1940, some eight million people from Holland, Belgium, and France fled south to escape from the anticipated battle zones. Most of them returned to their home towns after the fall of Paris.

Klaus Barbie (1913-1991) — "the Butcher of Lyon." Based in Lyon as chief of the German secret state police (Gestapo) for Vichy-France, he supervised the torture and murder of members of the Résistance and the deportation of Jews, altogether at least 850 persons. He was tried in 1987 for crimes against humanity in 177 cases and sentenced to life imprisonment.

Maquisard — a member of the Résistance. The term derives from "maquis" (scrub, underbrush).

Maurice Richard (1912-1944) — a captain in the Forces Françaises Libres (F.F.L.).

Dr. Eugene Minkovski (1885, in St. Petersburg – 1972) — a psychologist. He and his staff of five found hiding places for over 600 Jewish children in the countryside around Paris. Jenny Masour-Ratner (1895-1983) was one of his collaborators.

Chapter 10

Bruno Kurzweil (1891-1942) — a noted Jewish attorney from Graz who frequently represented socialists in court. He, his wife, Gisela, and their daughter, Adele (born in 1925), fled to France in October of 1938. They were handed over to the Gestapo in August 1942 and deported to Auschwitz.

Septfonds — in the département of Tarn-et-Garonne, housed approximately 1,500 Spanish refugees and, from February of 1941, other foreigners the authorities considered "non-dangerous."

Gurs — the harshest of the French detention centers, located fifty miles from the Spanish border in the département of Pyrénées Atlantiques. The camp was established in April 1939 to process anti-Franco Spaniards, nearly 19,000 of whom passed through Gurs during the following weeks. One year later, Gurs had 2,293 long-term inmates, whose number soon increased to 12,680. Most of them were women and children. During the winter of 1940/41, some 800 deaths occurred. The total number of prisoners who died at Gurs is 1,187. Between August 6, 1942 and the fall of 1943, about 6,000 Jewish prisoners were deported from Gurs to Auschwitz and Sobibór.

Chapter 11

Second International — an international alliance of socialist and labor parties (1881-1916) that, following its reorganization in 1920, merged with the International Working Union of Socialist Parties (IWUSP) to form the Social Democratic Labor and Socialist International, which existed until 1940.

The Jewish Labor Committee — was organized in New York City in 1934 to represent Jewish trade union interests.

The Emergency Rescue Committee — was founded in New York City on June 25, 1940, to rescue prominent artists and intellectuals who were stranded in southern France. Its representative in Marseille was Varian Fry, who used his Centre Américain de Secours until June 2, 1942, when it was forced to close, to obtain (sometimes forged) visas and other travel documents for his clients. By the end of July 1941, Fry had helped to facilitate the emigration of some 600 persons and had aided some 3,500 others in their efforts to leave France.

Muriel Gardiner (1901-1985) — was a medical student in Vienna. There she met Joseph Buttinger (1906-1992), who was elected Secretary of Austria's Social Democratic Party in 1930. She shared his exile in France and married him on August 1, 1939. See her book *Code Name "Mary": Memoirs of an American Woman in the Austrian Underground (1983)*. After 1946 she worked as a child psychiatrist in New York City.

Gilberto Bosques (1892-1995) — in 1940 the Mexican Consul General in Marseille. His office made possible the emigration to Mexico of more than 40,000 anti-Franco Spaniards and of many socialists and communists from central Europe.

Lázaro Cárdenas (1895-1970) — During his six years as president of Mexico (1934-1940), Cárdenas instituted various reforms.

Hicem — an organization founded in 1927 through the amalgamation of three groups: HIAS (Hebrew Sheltering and Immigrant Aid Society) in New York, ICA (Jewish Colonization Association) in Paris, and EMIGDIREKT in Berlin. Its office in Paris was transferred to Lisbon on June 26, 1940.

Chapter 12

Hanna Papanek (born 1927) — Ernst Papanek's daughter-in-law, was a member of a Berlin family that was active in social-democratic politics. After Hitler's assumption of power, they had to flee, first to Prague, then to Paris, and in 1940 to New York. In the United States, she became a prominent ethnologist and anthropologist.

Chapter 13

Pau — a city (now of 80,000) in the Béarn region (département de Pyrénées Atlantiques). Canfranc is a small Spansh border town.

Bacalhao — salted codfish.

Mis primeros pinitos . . . (My first steps in Spanish) — during the 1930s a popular primer for foreigners learning Spanish.

Chapter 14

Brígida (or: Brigitte) Alexander (1911 Stuttgart – 1995 Mexico City) — a writer and producer for television and the stage. Her first major TV series, *Los ángeles de la calle* (Street Angels), was aired from 1952 until 1955. The part of Aunt Mary in the motion picture *Like Water for Chocolate* (1992) made her famous as an actress. Her daughter Susana also became a film star.

Paul Westheim (1886-1963) — was a prolific German art historian, who, in 1950, published a major study of ancient religious art in Mexico, *Arte Antiguo de México*.

Laurette Séjourné (1911-2003) — was a noted French archeologist and ethnologist.

Gertrude Kurz (1906-1989) — was a professor of cybernetics at the Autonomous National University of Mexico.

Arnaldo Orfila (1897-1976).

The Immigrant (1917) — by and with Charles Chaplin.

Karl Dönitz (1891-1980) — the commander of the German submarine fleet (1936-1943) and, as of January 1943, in charge of all German naval operations. His strategy in the Battle of the Atlantic (1940-1943) entailed the concentrated use of U-boats ("wolf pack" tactics).

Bruno Traven (1882-1969) — a notoriously elusive author, lived in Mexico for close to fifty years and died in Mexico City. His novel *The Death Ship: The Sstory of an American Seaman* (1934) was first published in German in 1926.

Minyan ("number") — the group of ten adult Jewish men whose presence is required before public prayers in the synagogue can take place.

El Malecón — the coastal road in Havana.

Jarocho — a person, specifically a musician in the traditional white suit and hat, from Veracruz.

Chapter 15

Moctezuma II (ca.1465-1520) — ruled the Aztec empire from 1502 until his defeat by Hernán Cortés.

Pico de Orizaba (Citlatépetl, the Mountain of the Stars) — in the state of Puebla, at 18,707 ft. Mexico's highest mountain.

Marianne Frenk-Westheim (1898-2004) — the wife of the art historian Paul Westheim, was a renowned translator of German literature into Spanish.

Pepenador — a person who rummages through garbage dumps in search of things that could still be used.

Bundist — originally a member of the socialistic Bund, an organization founded in 1897 that helped Yiddish-speaking workers in Russia and Poland.

Red carnation — the international symbol of socialistic solidarity.

Sopa seca (dry soup) — a plate of rice or pasta.

Charro suit — the typical garment of Mexican horsemen.

Avenida de los Insurgentes — a major north-south thoroughfare in Mexico City.

Coyoacán — a southern suburb of the city where a large number of Mexican and foreign artists and intellectuals live.

Alvaro Obregón (1879-1915) — a general in the revolution of 1910 and president of the country from 1920 until 1924.

Monosabio — a cleanup worker in bullfight arenas.

Don Porfirio Diaz (1830-1915) — Mexico's dictatorial president from 1880 until 1911.

Miravalle — a noble family who traces its ancestry as far back as the marriage of Moctezuma's daughter Isabel Xipaguazin and Juan Cano de Saavedra.

Chingar — a swearword. Octavio Paz wrote a philosophical analysis of it in an essay in his collection *The Labyrinth of Solitude* (New York: Grove Press, 1985), pp. 73-88.

Air squadron — the elite Escuadrón 201 flew reconnaissance missions in the Gulf of Mexico and in 1945 over the Philippines. After the declaration of war against the axis powers and Japan on May 22, 1942, Mexico did not recruit a military force of its own but allowed 15,000 of its citizens to serve in the United States army.

Avila Camacho (1897-1955) — president from 1940 until 1946.

Chapter 16

Tin-Tan — stage name of Germán Valdés (1915-1983).

Nájera (1859-1895) — one of Mexico's most accomplished modernist writers.

Sierra (1848-1912) — a renowned poet and politician.

de Bucareli y Ursúa (1717-1779) — viceroy of New Spain (1771-1779).

Cristeros — Catholic opponents of the 1910 revolution, specifically objecting to the separation of church and state. In 1926, their movement instigated an armed insurrection that turned into a bloody civil war.

de la Huerta (1881-1955) — Mexican president in 1920. He lived in exile in the United States (1924-1935) until his rehabilitation by Lázaro Cárdenas.

Kisch, Seghers, et al. — prominent communist intellectuals and functionaries who, in 1941, founded the cultural organization, Heinrich Heine-Club, and a periodical, *Freies Deutschland/Alemania Libre*, and, on May 10, 1942, a publishing venture, *El Libro Libre*, whose first title was a collection of autobiographical sketches and reports by Egon Erwin Kisch (1885-1948), *Marktplatz der Sensationen*. It sold about 2,000 copies in a few months. (An American translation, *Sensation Fair*, had been published in 1941 by Modern Age Books in New York). *Das siebte Kreuz. Roman aus Hitlerdeutschland* (1943), a novel by Anna Seghers (1900-1983) about the escape of seven inmates from a concentration camp, appeared in January of 1943. Its American translation – *The Seventh Cross*

(Boston: Little, Brown, 1942) – became a bestseller and in 1944 was made into a commercially successful film.

Xitle — the cone of an extinct volcano on the southern periphery of Mexico City.

Roald Amundsen (1872-1928) — Norwegian explorer who reached the South Pole in 1911.

Stephens and Catherwood — John Lloyd Stephens (1805-1852) and Frederick Catherwood (1799-1854).

Labná — an important Mayan center in Yucatán.

Cacahuamilpa — near Taxco in the state of Guerrero, southwest of Mexico City.

ARAM — an organization (1942-1947) of Austrians exiled in Mexico that published the journal *Austria Libre*.

Chapter 17

Yonke — junk yard.

Anenecuilco — the birthplace of the revolutionary leader Emiliano Zapata (1879-1919).

Jarano — a tall, ornate sombrero.

Chapter 18

Pascual Orozco (1882-1915) — a famous general in the revolution of 1910.

Pelón ("shaved head") — a soldier who remained loyal to the government.

Comal — a griddle.

Chapter 19

Toledano (1894-1968) and Velázquez (1900-1997) — Mexican politicians and union leaders

L. Gregory (identification uncertain) — possibly Liddy Gregori, the wife of a Viennese actor and theater manager, Ferdinand Gregori.

James Matthew Barrie (1860-1937) — the creator of Peter Pan. *Rosalinde*, his one-act play for three actors, premiered in 1912.

Charles Rooner — stage name of the actor and director Ernst Robitschek (1901-1954). He and his wife, Luise Rooner, were major advocates of German-language theater in Mexico. He also appeared in numerous films, usually in the role of the dastardly villain.

Stanislavski — the professional name of Konstantin Sergeyevich Alekseyev (1863-1938), a theatrical pioneer and co-founder of the Moscow Art Theatre in 1898, who introduced a naturalistic style of acting that required the complete identification of the performers with the "inner truth" of the characters they portrayed.

Ayn Rand (1905-1982) — Her play, a courtroom drama in which the audience renders the verdict, was first produced under the title *Woman on Trial* in 1934.

Gogol (1809-1852) — The text *From a Madman's Diary: A Monologue* was arranged by Eric Bentley.

Pelota vasca — a game in which two or more players take turns hitting a hard rubber ball against a wall.

Johnny Weissmuller (1904-1984) — a champion swimmer (five Olympic gold medals) turned actor, who, between 1932 and 1948, played the role of Tarzan the Ape Man in twelve movies and appeared in sixteen *Jungle Jim* movies.

Morado (1909-2002).

Festival Cervantes — since 1995 an annual festival of the arts in Guanajuato, some 160 miles northwest of Mexico City.

Pulque — fermented agave juice.

Posada (1851-1913), Siqueiros (1896-1974), Rivera (1886-1957), José Joaquín Quirico Marcelino Clausell (1866-1935).

Loma Linda — a restaurant with a central dance floor.

El Gran Vals — i.e., *The Great Waltz* (1938*),* a movie with Luise Rainer, Fernand Garvet, and the coloratura soprano Miliza Korjus (1909-1980), directed by Julien Duvivier and Josef von Sternberg.

El Libro Negro del Terror Nazi en Europa. Testimonios de escritores y artistas de 16 naciones — (with 50 drawings and 164 photos), published by *El Libro Libre* in April 1943.

Lagów-Opatów — an extermination camp in the district of Lublin in Poland.

Richard Tauber (1891-1948), emigrated to London in 1938, and Joseph Schmidt (1904-1942, in the Swiss internment camp of Girenbad). — Both were very popular tenors who performed in operas, musicals, and movies.

Chapter 21

The Living Brain (1953) — a neurological study by W. Grey Walter, written for the general reader. It was published in Mexico by Editorial Fondo de Cultura Económica as *El Cerebro Viviente.*

Duet for One — by the English actor and playwright Tom Kempinski (born 1938), was first produced at the Bush Theatre in London in 1980. It is the story (akin to that of the English cellist Jacqueline du Pré, 1945-1987) of a talented violinist, Stefanie Abrahams, who is stricken with multiple sclerosis. Schwebel portrayed her physician, Dr. Alfred Feldmann.

Rosete Aranda — a puppet-theater group founded in 1835 by the brothers Josilián and Hermenegildo Rosete Aranda, active until 1943. Its most memorable characters were Vale Coyote, a campesino, and the arrogant matron, Doña Pascarroncita Mastuerzo de Verdega y Panza de Res y Gayverde.

Pita Amor — pen name of the poet Guadalupe Teresa Amor Schmidtlein (1918-2000).

India María — the stage name of María Elena Velasco (born 1940), a comic actress and movie director. *Ni de aquí ni de allá* (1987) is an adventure-comedy directed and co-written by her.

The Balcony (*Le balcon*, 1956; revised edition, 1962; English translation, 1966) — a satirical farce by Jean Genet (1910-1986).

Chapter 22

Huipil — a type of cotton shirt.

Chapter 24

Nauyaca — in Mexico also called *sorda*, a long poisonous snake.

Cabrón sabihondo — "you stupid know-it-all."

Chapter 25

El hombre mediocre (1913; The Average Man) — an "essay on psychology and morals" by the Italo-Argentine physician and sociologist José Ingenieros (1877-1925).

Chapter 26

Los Tuxtlas — a region south of the city of Veracruz.

Les Misérables (1862) — novel by Victor Hugo.

d'Artagnan — a young nobleman who strives to become a musketeer in Alexandre Dumas's novel, *The Three Musketeers* (1844).

Chingao — a derogatory term: "screwed-up."

Alvarado — a coastal town, notorious for the vulgar language of its inhabitants.

Chapter 27

Picho — blackbird.

Huarache — crude sandal made from old car tires.

Tórtola — turtledove.

Chapter 28

Mazate — comes from "Mazatl" (Nahuatl for "deer").

Tepezcuintle — huge rat-like mammal.

Chachalaca — small water bird.

Chapter 29

Zarzuela — a type of musical comedy, very popular in Spain and South America.

Green Ice (1981) — a movie about emerald smugglers, with Ryan O'Neal, Anne Archer, and Omar Sharif.

Chapter 30

Ferdinand Georg Waldmüller (1793-1865) — Viennese painter in the Biedermeier style.

Friedensreich Regentag Dunkelbunt Hundertwasser (1928-2000) — painter and sculptor.

Kapuzinergruft — the crypt, from 1633 until 1916, of seventeen Habsburg emperors and of fifteen empresses in the vault of the Capuchin Church.

Floridsdorf — Vienna's XXI. District, the largest and second most populous of its 23 districts.

Andreas Hofer (1767-1810, by firing squad) — a reputed Tyrolean patriot and freedom fighter who, in 1809, defeated a troop of Bavarians, Napoleon's allies, before being routed the following year by an army of 15,000.

Eugene, Prince of Savoy-Carignan (1663-1736) — imperial general, in his time Europe's most brilliant military strategist.

Joseph Wenzel, Count Radetzky (1766-1858) — the popular commander of Austrian forces in Northern Italy. *Radetzky-Marsch* was composed by Johann Strauss the Elder in 1848.

Oskar Kokoschka (1886-1980) — a versatile modernist painter.

Afterword

By Michael Winkler

Thoughtful readers tend to respond to a book of memoirs with scepticism, with an intuitive caution that they don't extend to other genres of autobiographical writing such as published diaries or collections of letters. This sense of unease is likely to be due to the realization that the memoirist must rely on the most capricious and unreliable of human faculties: memory. Bruno Schwebel's metaphor for this dilemma – "to unravel the tangle of my recollections" – can serve as a reminder that our memories are inchoate and often enough deceptive, that they fade and then vanish unless they are stimulated by persistent curiosity. They seldom return spontaneously or without continuous prompting.

But what makes this search for authenticity so important, especially for a person who lives the double life of an exile? And can a reader legitimately expect more from an exile's autobiography than an outline of basic facts and an appropriate degree of plausibility about most anything else? Schwebel suggests that the purpose of his at times obsessive and emotional probing into an inexorably receding past is the need to establish his own identity and to validate it ever anew. In the story "Mademoiselle de Fauche," he writes of his return, in 1981, to the farm where his father found work before their flight from France and where its owner, now ninety-three years old, still resides. He credits her, whom he imagines as having always lived in the past, with an "unbelievably sharp memory," quite in contrast to his own forgetfulness. But for all the pieces of information which she has accumulated and hoarded over the decades, she has no answer to the questions that are at the core of his autobiographical quest ("my pilgrimage"): who was I, what were we like?

Schwebel is a pertinacious but courteous inquirer and an observer with a keen eye for details. One could call this the scientific ("professional") side of his personality, which finds expression in a dry kind of humor and a laconic style of writing. Its complement – his artistic side – is characterized by the importance that sensory impressions have for him. He remembers something he tasted, smelled, touched, or heard and saw much more clearly and longer than the thoughts that he or others may have had at the time. And there is a part of him that is subject to overpowering, even debilitating emotions so that, at moments of high affective intensity, words fail him. Even so, his search for a credible identity has yielded a remarkably complex and subtle account.

Any writer who writes about himself also writes for himself and for those who are still or who were at one time closest to him. Memoirs, in other words, are also memorials or a form of testimonial on behalf of those who do not or who can no longer speak for themselves. Perhaps that is the reason so many of these people are mentioned by name – especially in the descriptions of the happy times in Neulengbach – when a general or collective phrase like "our large family" would be insufficient to suggest the role every single individual played in what soon would be a "lost childhood." And this loss, probably more than the pull of nostalgia, justifies the inclusion of family photos.

A book, of course, also tries to reach an audience of strangers. In Schwebel's case, this audience is primarily Mexican and Austrian (including German) readers, who are likely to approach him from entirely different vantage points. Consequently, he must write from a double perspective, which requires all the more discretion since his attitude toward both countries is a little more ambivalent than he may want to admit, at least publicly. Mexico, to be sure, did not become an interim domicile or an exilic ghetto for him, and he acknowledges with deep gratitude that country's hospitality. But he also acknowledges, *sotto voce*, his unalterable European mentality and his frustrated attempts to live out his life in Vienna.

Schwebel's chronicle of his life is noticeably free of emotionalized attitudes. But one may also get the impression that he is reticent to write in some detail about personal relationships – an observation that does not mean to question his right to keep private matters private. Nonetheless, his unceasing fascination with the beauty of Mexico's many landscapes does not seem to extend to its equally diverse people. It is almost as if he prefers not to describe any individual encounter directly, eye to eye, as it were, but as filtered through and refracted by the poetic imagination. For this reason, the nine stories that deal with particular Mexican characters do not distract from the autobiography's implicit purpose but supplement it, perhaps suggesting also that they constitute its earliest beginnings.

At any rate, the ten stories included in this volume have been published before, albeit in slightly different versions, in: Bruno Schwebel, *Comida corrida y otros cuentos*. México D.F.: Fontamara, 2004. The Spanish text of his memoirs, *De Viena a México – La otra suerte*, has also been published recently, in a handsome edition printed in 2006 for his *alma mater*, the Instituto Politécnico Nacional in Mexico City. This is not the text, however, on which this American translation is based. Rather, I have used only the German-language version titled *Das andere Glück. Erinnerungen und Erzählungen,* Wien: Theodor Kramer Gesellschaft, 2004, translated "with the help of the author and of Diethild Starkmeths by Jutta Lupprich" and with annotations (*Glossar*) by the editors, Christian Kloyber and Karl Müller. I was able to consult the original text only during the final stage of revising some locutions that still sounded not quite accurate or clear. Bruno Schwebel graciously helped me with a good number of suggestions and much factual information. He also provided the book's title. I am equally grateful to Barbara Gable of Ariadne Press who gave the entire typescript a careful reading and was especially helpful in matters of punctuation and layout. For the shortcomings of this translation of a translation, I alone accept full responsibility.